about the author

A musician and musicologist by profession, Lucy Robinson's energy and creativity are evident in her joyful, eclectic approach to cooking. Determined to eat well despite severe food intolerances, over the course of thirty years she has gathered together an impressively broad repertoire of recipes that exclude grains and meat. Inspired by flavours from around the globe, Lucy shares her delicious dishes with family and friends at her homes in Wales and France – and now, she shares them in this, her first book.

Cookery, France and music are three themes that have run through Lucy's life and inspired her, rooted in experiences such as childhood holidays in the Dordogne (memorably, eating a whole truffle *en croûte* in Quercy when she was 12) and the excitement of Debussy's *Pelléas et Mélisande* at Covent Garden. Going on to study Music at York University, she wrote her PhD at Cambridge and, in the course of her research, spent a year in Paris, which proved an inspiring environment for her expanding culinary tastes.

As a musician, Lucy plays the viola da gamba and has performed in venues ranging from the Wigmore Hall in London to the Sydney Opera House. History and research are a passion: when preparing for a performance, Lucy likes to get under the skin of the piece's composer – including pondering on what they read and ate. Similarly, in assembling the recipes for this book, she was drawn to research the stories behind the dishes and their ingredients. As Head of Postgraduate Studies and Research at the Royal Welsh College of Music and Drama, Lucy enjoyed connecting with the cultures – and cuisine – of her international students, from places as widespread as Catalonia, Iran and China.

Lucy is married to the composer Andrew Wilson-Dickson. She has three children from her previous marriage: Sam, a cameraman, who took the photos for this book; Alex, a chef at Rochelle Canteen in London and a mine of culinary advice; and Louis, the family mathematician and curry specialist.

simple, delicious recipes
without meat or grains

the
grain-free
vegetarian

lucy robinson

photographs by samuel vines

FORQUERAY PRESS

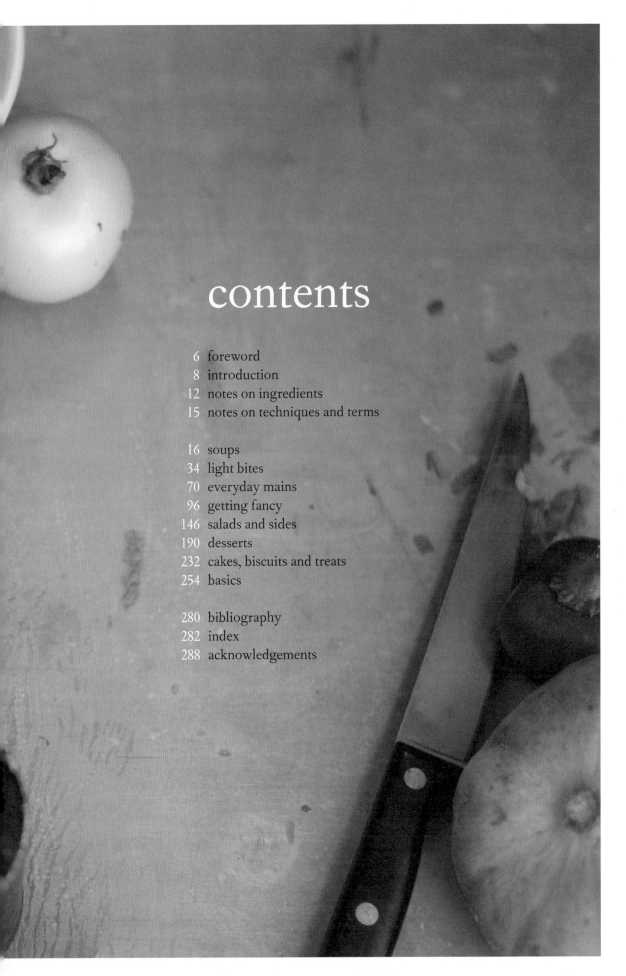

contents

foreword

When I was growing up, we didn't eat like any other family I knew. While my friends' mums were serving up burgers, oven chips and frozen peas, my mother Lucy, the author of this book, was providing us with spinach roulade or globe artichokes with aïoli. At times, my mates would laugh at me for the 'weird' food that arrived on their plates whenever they ate at my house. And yes, in primary school, there were times when I wanted to fit in and have the breadcrumbed food served for school dinners, but the food I ate at home was delicious, and I realised I was lucky to have it.

As I grew older, I came to understand that one reason for our unusual diet was Mum's food intolerances. Before we were born, she had discovered that she was intolerant of grains and cane sugar, and had realised how unwell meat made her feel. Impressively, instead of letting this restrict her diet, she turned it into an opportunity to experiment with all sorts of different ingredients and flavours. Her intolerance of pesticides encouraged her to arrange deliveries of organic vegetables from local farmers long before this was trendy or commonplace (again, my friends thought this was pretty bizarre).

It was Mum's enthusiasm for food that inspired me to become an adventurous cook. I still use cookery books with inscriptions from her on the inside, like 'Happy Thirteenth Birthday'. Growing up, I would frequently help to knock up dinners for thirty plus students or for a whole orchestra before a concert. I saw how much satisfaction could be got from feeding grateful and hungry people, and this inspired me in my twenties to pursue a career as a chef.

Not only did Lucy teach me to cook, she also encouraged me to think about the provenance of food and, in 2012, I completed a Masters degree in Food Policy. Interestingly, the knowledge I gained on this course complemented Mum's philosophy of cooking and eating – acknowledging the benefits of using fresh, seasonal produce that has been locally sourced or even home grown. This approach guarantees delicious food and has the least negative impact on our fragile planet.

This book isn't just about coping with allergies or about strictly vegetarian cooking. It's a way of thinking about food and taking control of your diet. It's about being conscious of what goes onto your plate and what this means for you and the planet, while enjoying and sharing delicious meals. My Mum's style of cooking has influenced me greatly and I hope that, through this book, she can inspire you too.

Alex Vines

introduction

Thirty years ago, after years of unexplained symptoms, I made some important discoveries about my body: that I am deeply intolerant of all grains (including sugar derived from sugar cane, which is a grain); that my body is not good with meat and cow products, but it can cope with butter (which is virtually free from protein, the trigger to my symptoms) and small amounts of organic cream and organic Parmesan; and that I am sensitive to petrochemicals, including those sprayed on fruits and vegetables.

These discoveries made it clear that, in order to stablise my health, I had to become a vegetarian and avoid the dietary 'offenders'. This might have been a culinary life-sentence, condemning me to a severely restricted diet, but I've always been an adventurous eater and saw the situation as an opportunity to experiment with new ways of cooking and eating. This exciting new challenge fired me up to learn how to use a new palette of tastes and textures to bring out the best of their flavours, and I have never looked back.

The detection of my food intolerances literally changed my life – I burst out of a world of depression and lethargy into a life of joy and energy. Most importantly at the time, I could finish my PhD – which I wrote up in just three months. So enchanted was I by the potential of my new-found friends – vegetables, fruits, goat and sheep cheeses, nuts, raw honey, all flavoured with herbs and spices – that it never crossed my mind to miss foods like bread. (After all, if you need carbohydrate, what could be more satisfying than a potato!) I had found a new way to eat and it was a great pleasure to gather and create recipes that celebrated the wonderful foods that nourished me.

My family and friends were supportive and rose to the challenge of conceiving delicious 'Lucy-proof' recipes for us to share, some of which are included in this book. I vividly remember the exquisite dinner that chef David Adlard cooked for me at this time in his restaurant in Wymondham, deftly negotiating my unusual requirements. He was later to hold a Michelin star for nearly 20 years. It became clear that my dietary restrictions did not in any way have to stop me from enjoying a broad and even gourmet-quality diet.

Having incorporated my requirements into the daily cooking routine for my family, and in the feeding of students and friends, I've seen clearly that this sort of diet is beneficial and enjoyed by all who have come into contact with it. I haven't had to re-invent, experiment with substitutes, or brainstorm outlandish new recipes from scratch – I've simply drawn on the wealth of the world's cooking, incorporating dishes that have a long history and have stood the test of time simply because they are so enjoyable and achievable.

For me, food is about love, creativity, generosity, sharing and conversation. So my top priority is to share the best possible food, which means using really fresh ingredients, and choosing food that is free from pesticides and other contaminants. Seeking out the best food also means buying produce that has been grown ethically and, whenever possible, locally. One solution to this quest is to grow some food yourself. I enjoy cultivating my own fruits and vegetables and get enormous pleasure from watching my plants developing. I feel passionately that many more people could do this, albeit on a small scale. The more home-grown food we can produce, the more we can contribute to the reduction of the vast carbon footprint that results from transporting food around the world. Of course, it isn't possible to grow everything yourself, and an excellent source of fresh organic food is your local farmers' market.

I developed my love of markets as a child visiting the Dordogne. What a dazzling array of beautiful, sunny vegetables, fruits and cheeses were proudly presented by the local farmers! So it was a dream-come-true to buy a wreck of a house in the Tarn, restore it and live part of the year in the little French village of Marnaves. In France, I've been able to indulge my natural inclination for Mediterranean food and I've picked up all sorts of tips from the locals, not least about preserving vegetables for the winter. And our neighbours, who come from a seriously meaty tradition, are remarkably open-minded about sitting down to aubergine cannelloni and *kibriʒli* cake, and then afterwards asking for the recipes.

My way of eating naturally keeps you slim, but it doesn't mean you have to go without desserts. I relish making cakes and desserts using ground almonds, fruits or, sometimes, chocolate and raw artisan honey. For a musician it is essential to be mentally and physically fit. I often play the viola da gamba for hours and I find that the fibre-rich foods and slow-burning proteins of my diet provide me with the sustained energy I need. (And I always keep a stock of organic dried apricots and almonds to hand to stave off any hunger pangs!)

And as a musician, I have been immensely fortunate in having some highly gifted teachers who, as well as passing on their musical culture, would often invite me to eat with them. When I studied at the Brussels Conservatoire with the viol-player Wieland Kuijken, he would regularly invite all his students round for a meal with his wife and seven children, which we hugely appreciated. So when I started teaching myself, it was natural to me to follow the tradition and invite my students back home for Sunday lunch *en famille*. They appeared to enjoy my fresh approach to food and started to suggest that I should write a cookery book. Later generations became more persuasive and I promised that I would write one as soon as I finished working full time. So, here it is – the result of many years of experimenting, learning and perfecting recipes. This book is designed for those who share all or some of my intolerances, or for those who, for reasons of health, ethics or purely personal preference, are looking for meat-free recipes, want to consume fewer carbohydrates or grains for a more balanced diet, or for anyone simply interested in fresh, natural, healthy and delicious food. I hope you enjoy cooking – and sharing – the recipes as much as I have.

notes on ingredients

One of the great joys of cooking is the extraordinary variety that nature provides to inspire us. However, recipes go against nature's diversity by attempting to tie things down that cannot be tied down, such as the size of a lemon and its juiciness. Thus, instinct – sharpened by experience and supported by the use of all five senses – must play its part in the interpretation of recipes. I hope the information below will also help you to produce some delicious meals.

ALMONDS These will burn if cooked above 170°C.

BAKING POWDER Most commercial baking powder includes wheat. Use one part bicarbonate of soda to two parts of cream of tartar as an alternative, to be safely wheat-free. The cream of tartar provides the acidity to make the bicarbonate of soda react to produce CO_2. Thus, when a recipe already includes an acid, such as orange, use bicarbonate of soda alone.

BUCKWHEAT 'Saracen corn', as it is known in France and Italy, is a member of the sorrel and dock family and is extremely hardy, growing fast on poor soil and in cold climates. It became a peasant staple in Brittany, as well as in countries of the former Soviet Union and the mountainous regions of Japan. The English word 'buckwheat' is borrowed from the Dutch *bockweit* meaning, literally, 'beechwheat' because its curiously shaped little seeds (known as groats) were thought to resemble beech nuts. Buckwheat groats are often roasted or ground into flour.

CEPS *Boletus edulis* mushrooms. Porcini is the Italian name for ceps. The seven dark mushrooms shown on page 96 are ceps.

CHICKPEA FLOUR Also known as *besan*, gram flour and garbanzo bean flour. Easily available at Indian shops, in supermarkets or online.

DAIRY PRODUCTS I use goats' and sheep's milk, cheese and yogurt – artisan made, organic and unpasteurised. I use unsalted organic cows' butter, and cook with organic double cows' cream. Thus, when I write 'milk' as an ingredient in my recipes, I use goats' milk. Remember that Greeks soak their feta and halloumi in water for 12 hours to draw out the salt used as a preservative; you might like to do the same.

KAFFIR LIME LEAVES These are essential for Thai food. They are to be found, frozen and fresh, in Chinese and Asian supermarkets.

HERBS I love using fresh herbs in my cooking and salads. I grow chives, coriander leaves, fennel, horseradish (in an old china sink), lavender, lemon-scented geranium, lemon verbena, lovage, mint, oregano, flat-leaf parsley, rosemary, sage, sorrel, tarragon, thyme and wild garlic close to the house so that they are handy. Many of them have pretty flowers, too, which I use for decorating salads along with nasturtium and pansy flowers, as well as rose petals.

HONEY I use raw artisan honey from producers I know. As ever with nature, there is remarkable variety. I like to have a gentle one, like sunflower, and a fragrant one, such as chestnut, to complement different ingredients. One characteristic of raw honey is that it starts to solidify after a few months; when I make vinaigrette I warm it up until it is liquid before adding it to the other ingredients. Honey burns if cooked above 170°C.

LEMONS I use untreated organic citrus fruit.

MARIGOLD BOUILLON Of course, you achieve the best results for a soup by creating a stock made from fresh vegetables (onions, carrots, leeks, fennel and celery) but most of us do not have the time. I use gluten-free Marigold Swiss Vegetable bouillon. The trick is to give flavouring without making all your soups taste of Marigold bouillon so I generally use about 2 teaspoons per litre of water.

OLIVE OIL I buy high-quality, organic extra virgin olive oil in bulk from Essential Trading (www.essential-trading.coop). Olive oil is so central to my cooking that I generally use this organic olive oil whenever I need it. (I also buy my dry and tinned food from Essential Trading because they support fair trade, are sensitive to the environment and sell a wide range of organic foods.)

PARSLEY I prefer the stronger-tasting Continental flat-leaf parsley.

PEPPERS In Britain I generally use Romano peppers because I find they are much sweeter and more flavoursome than the bell peppers, which often have not received enough sun. Around the Mediterranean the bell peppers are properly ripened and are wonderfully sweet.

POTATO FLOUR Potato starch flour is found easily and cheaply in Indian shops (where it is often called *farina*), in supermarkets supplying Indian ingredients or online. Potato flour is a very fine white powder. It has a similar texture to cornflour (or cornstarch, as it is called in the United States) – and is made from dried potato starch. It has a neutral flavour. In the US it is called potato starch.

PRESERVED LEMONS Use the chopped, rinsed lemon rind only.

SEASONING For salt, I use Maldon sea salt on salads and at the table because the crystals are lighter and not as strong as French sea salt, which I use for cooking. I freshly grind black peppercorns and I often use a pestle and mortar for larger quantities. Nutmeg is also always freshly grated. Lemon is often used as a seasoning 'to taste' in Indian and Mediterranean recipes. I replace the Indian jaggery (commercially commonly made from sugar cane) with honey.

TAHINI Choose a light variety from a Middle Eastern shop.

TOMATOES I do not hesitate to sweeten tomatoes in Britain with a little honey if they are out of season and tasteless. Often, a better alternative is to use organic canned tomatoes, which hold the sunny sweetness from when and where they have been canned.

SPICES I buy my spices in an Indian or Middle Eastern shop as I find these are generally fresher, tastier, significantly cheaper and more appropriately packaged than their supermarket equivalents.

VINEGAR I used to find vinegar too acidic and avoided it. But the discovery of Catalan artisan vinegars has completely changed my view. Castell de Gardeny Riesling vinegar is fantastic alongside lemon juice in vinaigrette and moves mayonnaise onto a new level.

notes on techniques and terms

AL DENTE Literally, 'to the tooth', meaning just cooked and still quite firm and crunchy.

BLANCH When a vegetable, fruit or nut is blanched it is immersed for a short time in boiling water. Sometimes, but not necessarily, it is also 'refreshed' by briefly plunging it into iced water, which stops it from cooking further.

BAIN-MARIE A bain-marie is a bath of hot water into which is placed a dish containing the food to be cooked, then the entire set-up is put into the oven to allow the food to cook gently. This technique is excellent for cooking custards as it makes them tender and prevents them from curdling. I use a roasting pan with moderately high sides to create a bain-marie. I fill it with boiling water until it comes two thirds up the side of the ramekin or serving dish that contains the food.

CRUSHED I have used the term 'crushed' to describe crushing a seed or nut in a mortar with a pestle.

DRY-ROAST This involves applying heat to nuts, seeds, spices or flour without using water or oil, to enhance their flavour. Use a stainless steel or cast iron pan and constantly stir so that they turn golden evenly.

MANDOLINE This is an invaluable tool for slicing vegetables for salads. Do use the hand protector!

OVEN TEMPERATURES I have given these for a fan-assisted ovens.

PARBOIL This means to partially boil. The cooking is usually finished by another means, such as grilling or frying.

POTATO RICER This ingenious gadget – like a giant garlic press for boiled potatoes – makes amazingly smooth mashed potatoes with little effort. It is also excellent for making pumpkin gnocchi.

ROASTING/TOASTING NUTS Delia Smith's fail-safe formula for roasting nuts in the oven is 170°C for 8 minutes.

SAUTÉ French for 'jumped', meaning the food is tossed around in a pan in a little oil over a high heat.

TEMPER This term refers to the process of frying whole spices – such as mustard, cumin or fenugreek seeds – in hot oil until they splutter and burst, which takes about 1 minute. This mellows their flavour and releases it into the oil.

SOUPS

gazpacho

This exhuberantly colourful chilled Andalusian soup is just the thing for a sizzling Mediterranean day. The secret of success is to find deep red, wonderfully sweet sun-ripened tomatoes, although a Catalan friend adds some Charentais melon to increase its sweetness.

SERVES 6

1 red pepper, roughly chopped
1.5kg ripe tomatoes, roughly chopped
½ sweet melon (such as a Charentais), skinned (optional)
3 garlic cloves, roughly chopped
1 green chilli, deseeded and roughly chopped
8 tablespoons olive oil
5 tablespoons white wine or sherry vinegar
1 teaspoon cumin seeds
Salt and pepper
Honey
½ cucumber, cut into 1cm cubes
2 shallots or 1 small red onion, finely chopped
1 green pepper, finely chopped
Handful of parsley, leaves picked and finely chopped
8 ice cubes

In a food processor, blend the red pepper with a couple of handfuls of chopped tomato until smooth. Add the rest of the tomatoes, the melon, garlic, chilli, olive oil, vinegar and cumin seeds and blend until creamy, using a little water to thin the soup if necessary. Season. Add about 1 tablespoon honey if the tomatoes need sweetening.

Pour the soup into a large serving bowl and sprinkle the cucumber, shallots and green pepper over the top. Cover and chill in the fridge for 1 hour.

Add the parsley and ice cubes and serve.

VARIATION

If you like the soup thickened, use 3–4 tablespoons ground almonds, stirred in as you season the soup.

sorrel soup

Sorrel is a perennial garden herb that is easy to grow to add to salads, soups and sauces. Writer and gardener John Evelyn valued its vibrant lemony flavour for 'sharpning appetite' and 'imparting so grateful a quickness to the rest'; it was 'therefore never to be excluded' (*Acetaria, a Discourse on Sallets,* 1699). Renowned French chef La Varenne recommends using sorrel in soups in his celebrated cookery book, *Le Cuisinier François* (1651), and favours the combination of sorrel and eggs. Sorrel omelette cooked in butter makes a quick feast for an unexpected friend, as does a poached egg perched on a nest of sorrel – soften a couple of handfuls of sorrel in some butter and add a little crème fraîche. As with spinach, the leaves need careful cleaning and tough stalks should be removed before cooking. Do not be discouraged by the fact that sorrel goes brown when cooked.

This tasty soup can be served hot or chilled. If it is to be served chilled, do not reheat it after the cream has been added. It was my mother's brainwave to blitz the sorrel leaves uncooked.

SERVES 5–6

60g butter
8 large shallots or 2 large white onions, chopped
2 garlic cloves, chopped
1 litre hot vegetable stock, made with
  2 teaspoons Marigold bouillon powder
125ml cream
300g sorrel leaves, cleaned and roughly chopped
Salt and pepper
Nutmeg
Crème fraîche, to serve

Melt the butter in a large saucepan and cook the shallots and garlic gently until completely broken down, about 15 minutes. Add the stock and simmer for 5 minutes. Stir in the cream and bring to a simmer.

Take the pan off the heat and blitz the mixture with a hand-held blender. Add the raw sorrel and blitz as finely as you can. Season with salt, pepper and a grating of fresh nutmeg to taste and briefly bring to simmering point. Serve with a dollop of crème fraîche.

VARIATION

Watercress makes an excellent alternative to sorrel in this recipe, and can likewise be served hot or chilled.

catalan fennel soup

Catalonia's extraordinarily varied and colourful gastronomy can be traced back to its rich culture in the Middle Ages and Renaissance. At that time Catalonia stretched from Roussillon in the north to Alicante in the south and also included the Balearic Islands. In the late medieval period its empire also embraced Sicily, Sardinia, Naples and parts of Greece, with trading posts as far afield as North Africa and Alexandria. The Romans, who planted olives and vines, lived in Catalonia for over 600 years from the third century BC, followed by the Arabs, in the early eighth century, bringing with them their remarkable expertise in agriculture, notably irrigation, and new plants such as spinach, aubergine, Seville orange and saffron – all of which remain highly characteristic of Catalan cookery. For centuries, Catalan cuisine was the flagship for European tastes. Catalan cooks delight in mixing savoury with sweet and sweet with sour.

Seductively creamy, with a hint of orange, *sopa de fonoll* is one of my favourite soups – equally at home at the centre of a lunch with friends or as a starter for a dinner party. On a hot Mediterranean day *sopa de fonoll* is excellent served chilled; but check the consistency as you may need to add a little extra water.

SERVES 6

50g butter
2 shallots, chopped
1 garlic clove, chopped
900g fennel, trimmed and chopped, reserving some
  feathery fronds for decoration
Grated zest of 1 orange, plus extra to garnish
900ml hot vegetable stock, made with
  1½ teaspoons Marigold bouillon powder
125ml cream
Salt and pepper

Melt the butter in a large saucepan over a gentle heat and soften the shallots and garlic, about 15 minutes. Add the fennel and orange zest and cook for a further 10 minutes. Add the hot stock and bring to the boil. Reduce the heat, cover and simmer gently until the fennel is tender, about 20 minutes.

Take the pan off the heat and, using a hand-held blender, blend the mixture thoroughly until smooth. Stir in the cream and season. Reheat gently to serve, garnishing with the reserved feathery fennel fronds and grated orange zest.

celery and cashew nut soup

This enticingly creamy soup is perfect for a wintry lunch. Celery always reminds me of the delight of the new season's flavoursome arrival in Cambridge market, 'dirty' with the jet-black Fenland soil. Fen celery is now the first English vegetable to have received EU-protected status.

If you feel strongly about its stringy fibres, you can remove most of them by gently snapping the fleshy part of the stem and pulling them off. Or alternatively, take a potato peeler to the convex side of the stalk to peel away the fibres.

Velvety ground cashew nuts make an excellent alternative to potatoes for thickening soups. The practice of thickening with ground nuts, particularly almonds, dates back at least to the Middle Ages.

The Amazonian cashew tree is a member of the *Anacardiaceae* family, like the mango, sumac and pistachio. In the sixteenth century it was introduced to Goa by the Portuguese, and from there it spread throughout the Far East and to Africa. The Portuguese turned the native Tupi name of *acaju* into *caju*, whence the English 'cashew'. The cashew nut hangs at the base of a large red or orange fruit.

This recipe is inspired by the Celery and Cashew Nut Soup in *The New Covent Garden Soup Company's Book of Soups*, edited by Fiona Geddes.

SERVES 4

1 large head of celery
2 tablespoons olive oil
1 red onion, roughly chopped
3 garlic cloves, roughly chopped
100g cashew nuts, freshly ground
900ml hot vegetable stock, made with
    1½ teaspoons Marigold bouillon powder
Salt and pepper

Break off the individual sticks of celery from the head and chop finely, on the diagonal, to keep the characteristic celery fibres as short as possible.

Heat the oil in a large saucepan over a medium-low heat and soften the onion, garlic and celery, about 10 minutes. Stir in the ground cashew nuts and stock and simmer for 10 minutes.

Take the pan off the heat, blitz with a hand-held blender, season the soup and serve.

french onion soup

I had my first taste of this classic heart-warming soup when I lived in Paris whilst working on my thesis. A friend took me to one of the cafés surrounding what had been the central Parisian market, Les Halles, where the soup quietly simmered all night, ready for the ravenous traders. At the entrance to Les Halles stands the vast sixteenth-century church of Saint Eustache, where Molière was christened and Berlioz's *Te Deum* received its première in 1855. During the 1850s the architect Victor Baltard constructed magnificent glass and iron buildings for the market. In 1873, the hungry young Emile Zola described Les Halles as *le ventre de Paris* (the belly of Paris) in vivid detail in his novel of the name. Sadly Baltard's buildings were being demolished whilst I was sipping my first *soupe à l'oignon*.

The French AOC (*Appellation d'Origine Contrôlée*) onions, Pink Roscoff, famously brought to Britain by Breton farmers and sold plaited into tresses strung over their bicycles, are ideal for this soup. Red onions are wonderfully sweet, too.

SERVES 4

130g butter
2 tablespoons olive oil
850g onions, finely chopped
1.1 litres hot vegetable stock, made with
   1 tablespoon Marigold bouillon powder
300ml cider
1 sprig of thyme, leaves picked
40ml Calvados (optional)
Salt and pepper
140g Manchego or Pecorino cheese, grated

Melt the butter with a dash of olive oil (to reduce the risk of the butter burning) in a large saucepan and gently fry the onions until they start to caramelise, about 35 minutes. Add the stock, cider and thyme and simmer for 10 minutes. Then add the Calvados, if using. Season with salt and coarsely ground pepper pulverised using a pestle and mortar.

Set the grill to a medium heat. Ladle the soup into 4 ovenproof bowls. Spread the cheese over the soup and brown it under the grill. Serve.

VARIATION

For a dairy-free version, soften the onions in olive oil and omit the cheese finale.

cosy winter
weekend lunch

Light the wood fire, make merry and keep warm against the
sleet and snow outside with some good stories within. Try this
delicious warming lunch made from seasonal vegetables and
fruit. Creamy Tuscan bean soup is the centrepiece; it uses
cannellini beans, dried in the autumn, cooked with herbs and
garlic. Chicory is a winter salad leaf grown in abundance
in Belgium – when I studied there I lived on it all winter;
the orange crop begins in December and the year's walnuts
will have ripened and dried, too. Blackberry and apple
crumble, liberally sprinkled with flaked almonds,
makes a happy conclusion to the meal.

Bowl of Italian olives – such as Bella di
Cerignola, Nocellara del Belice or Taggiasca
– to welcome everyone *from the deli*

Tuscan Bean Soup *page 25*

Chicory, Orange and Walnut Salad *page 152*
with a plate of Italian cheese, perhaps Gorgonzola,
Pecorino and some nicely ripened Taleggio *from the deli*

Blackberry and Apple Crumble with
whipped cream *page 192 variation*

TO DRINK

An elegant Tuscan Chianti Classico and an aromatic
dry Pinot Grigio, with some artisan Bramley
and Cox apple juice to hand

tuscan bean soup

Zuppa di fagioli alla Toscana is a delicious, creamy soup to nourish and keep you warm in winter. In the autumn, if you are fortunate enough to find the new season's beans from the Mediterranean, they are the first choice, but any good-quality cannellini beans will make an excellent soup. Remember not to add salt to your soup until the beans are soft or the skins will not cook.

This recipe comes from Giovanna, a highly creative and generous cook and ex-student of ours who invited us out to Tuscany, where we sampled her parents' memorable bottled tomatoes, olive oil, red and white wine, *vin santo* and *limoncello*. Each wine bottle was opened with anticipation and everyone tasted a bit to assess its salient merits – it made the uniformity of commercial wine suddenly seem rather boring. The *Carabinieri* kept a friendly eye on the locals' ventures into distilling but, as long as they were given some to sample, no one bothered further.

SERVES 4

250g dried cannellini beans
900ml water
4 sage leaves
4 tablespoons olive oil
3 garlic cloves, chopped
1 sprig of rosemary
1 tomato, chopped
Salt and pepper

Soak the beans overnight in plenty of water. Drain and rinse. Cover the beans with the fresh water, add the sage leaves and 1 tablespoon olive oil and bring to the boil. Lower the heat and simmer until tender, 45 minutes to 1½ hours, depending on the freshness of the beans.

Meanwhile, heat 2 tablespoons oil in a saucepan and gently fry the garlic until golden with the sprig of rosemary, about 8 minutes. Add the tomato and fry until cooked, about 5 minutes.

Transfer half the beans to a medium-sized bowl with some of the bean stock. Blend with a hand-held blender, then return to the pan. Heat the soup, add the tomato. Season. Serve sprinkled with the remaining oil.

VARIATIONS

– Use haricot beans if you cannot find cannellini.
– Add 200g thinly shredded spinach to the soup when you put in the bean purée and simmer until the spinach has wilted.

quick courgette soup

Courgettes are wonderfully rewarding plants to grow. In our Cardiff garden I plant all our vegetables in amongst the old-fashioned roses, lilies and herbs. So I was delighted to discover that Louis XIV was so enamoured by the miraculous range of new vegetables available in France by the mid-seventeenth century that he, too, proudly mixed them with his herbaceous plants. The deep-yellow flowers of the courgette plant definitely hold their own amongst the more familiar garden blooms.

One of the joys of growing your own courgettes is that you can pick succulent young fruits (about 10cm long) and gently fry them in olive oil, perhaps with a little garlic, or pluck the flowers to eat (see page 52). Inevitably, I find some of the fruits manage to hide behind their enormous leaves and grow with great speed to a rather larger size than I had intended. These are the ones I use for this tasty soup.

SERVES 4

2 tablespoons olive oil
3 garlic cloves, chopped
600g courgettes, chopped
Handful of basil, leaves picked and roughly chopped
600ml hot vegetable stock, made with
    2 teaspoons Marigold bouillon powder
75ml cream
Salt and pepper

Heat the olive oil in a saucepan over a medium-low heat. Add the garlic, courgettes and basil and fry gently until the garlic and courgettes are light gold, about 10 minutes. Add the vegetable stock, bring to the boil, then simmer for about 10 minutes.

Using a slotted spoon, set aside a quarter of the courgettes in a bowl. Take the pan off the heat and blend the rest of the soup in the saucepan using a hand-held blender. Add the cream and blend briefly. Season to taste. Stir in the reserved courgettes. Serve hot.

quick pea soup

Peas come from the Middle East and were enjoyed by the ancient Greeks and Romans; soon afterwards they reached India and had found their way to China by the seventh century. Early peas were dried and were a staple food for poor people in Europe during the Middle Ages. In the sixteenth century, Italian gardeners bred a tender pea for eating immature and fresh. A taste for these succulenct young peas became a craze in England and France, prompting Louis XIV's favourite, Madame de Maintenon, to note with disdain in 1696: 'There are some ladies who, having eaten a hearty supper, risk indigestion by scoffing peas at home before going to bed. It's a fashion, all the rage'.

Whilst nothing matches peas picked straight from the garden – they lose their freshness quickly – modern techniques of freezing them within a couple of hours from harvesting are highly successful. A packet of petits pois in the freezer is handy for creating this delicate soup in about a quarter of an hour.

SERVES 4

3 tablespoons olive oil
1 large onion, roughly chopped
2 garlic cloves, roughly chopped
500g frozen petits pois
1 litre hot vegetable stock, made with
   1½ teaspoons Marigold bouillon powder
3 tablespoons chopped mint
100ml cream
Salt and pepper
Nutmeg

Heat the oil in a large saucepan over a medium-low heat and soften the onion and garlic, about 10 minutes. Add the peas and stock and bring to the boil. Simmer until the peas are soft, about 5 minutes.

Add 2 tablespoons of the mint, take the pan off the heat and blitz your soup with a hand-held blender. Stir in the cream and season with salt, pepper and a grating of nutmeg to taste. Briefly return the soup to the heat and bring it to simmering point to heat through. Serve garnished with the remaining chopped mint.

clear beetroot soup

In Poland, a vegetarian *barszcz* is served at the beginning of the *Wigilia* (Christmas Eve vigil) feast. Poles fast during Christmas Eve daytime then, traditionally, at dusk, the youngest child is sent outside to watch for the arrival of the first star. On its appearance, the family shares pieces of *oplatek* (Christmas wafer) and wish each other joy for the forthcoming year – a wish sealed with a kiss. In the country, pieces of *oplatek* are fed to the animals, too, because part of the tradition is that they speak with a human voice at midnight.

Although I have used lemon juice here, the traditional way to create the acidity is to make the soup three to four days in advance and let it sour naturally in a warm room. *Barszcz* is light, tasty and so pretty – a gorgeous way to start Christmas dinner.

SERVES 8–10

1.5kg beetroot, grated
½ teaspoon caraway seeds
2.5 litres hot vegetable stock, made with
   1 tablespoon Marigold bouillon powder
3 tablespoons lemon juice
3 tablespoons apple juice concentrate
Salt and pepper
Crème fraîche, to serve

Put the beetroot and caraway seeds in a large saucepan and cover with the hot stock. With a lid on, bring the stock to the boil, then simmer for 1½ hours.

Strain the soup through a sieve, discarding the beetroot and caraway seeds. Stir in the lemon juice and apple juice concentrate and season with salt and pepper. Reheat and serve drizzled with the crème fraîche.

VARIATIONS

– Serve chilled in summer. Leave the soup to cool to room temperature, then refrigerate for 1 hour before serving.
– Substitute 1 crushed allspice berry for the caraway seeds.

pumpkin soup with slow-roasted tomato cream

I have a passion for Crown Prince pumpkins; happily they are in season as the autumn days draw in, for which they make a magnificent warming soup. Once the frost bites, they should be stored indoors at a low temperature, but not below 6°C. By hoarding a clutch in the spare bedroom, I find I can extend their time until March – if I've amassed enough. Incidentally, the English word 'pumpkin' is believed to derive from the early French *pompon*, whereas the American 'squash' comes from the Massachusett Indian word *askutasquash*.

If you cannot find a steely-blue-skinned Crown Prince, use another firm, orange-fleshed pumpkin such as a butternut squash, but the flavour will not be as deep.

SERVES 6

4 tablespoons olive oil
2 large onions, chopped
2 garlic cloves, chopped
1kg pumpkin, peeled and chopped into chunks
1.5 litres hot vegetable stock, made with
    2 teaspoons Marigold bouillon powder
125ml cream
Salt and pepper
Nutmeg

SLOW-ROASTED TOMATO CREAM

100g Slow-roasted Tomatoes (see page 260), chopped
150ml cream

Preheat the grill on a medium-high setting.

Heat 2 tablespoons of the olive oil in a large saucepan over a medium-low heat and soften the onion and garlic, about 10 minutes.

Meanwhile, toss the pumpkin in the remaining olive oil and grill lightly, turning once, until the flesh is golden and soft on both sides, about 15 minutes. Add the pumpkin and stock to the onions and bring to the boil. Simmer until the pumpkin is soft, about 15 minutes.

While the soup is simmering, blend the slow-roasted tomatoes and cream in a food processor and set aside.

Take the soup off the heat and blend it using a hand-held blender. Add the cream and season with salt, pepper and a grating of nutmeg to taste. Serve with a dollop of slow-roasted tomato cream in each bowl.

thai tom yum pumpkin soup

Piquant chillies enhance the warming effect of this beautiful, aromatic soup. In Thai, *tom yum* refers to a hot, spicy and sour soup.

SERVES 4

750g pumpkin, peeled and
    chopped into bite-sized cubes
2 tablespoons sunflower oil
10 shallots, finely sliced
2 garlic cloves, finely chopped
1 teaspoon crushed dried chilli
1 small fresh red chilli, deseeded
    and finely chopped
½ teaspoon coriander seeds
½ teaspoon cumin seeds
1 tablespoon peanuts
1 teaspoon finely sliced
    lemongrass
1 teaspoon grated ginger root

3 Kaffir lime leaves
2 tablespoons water
500ml hot vegetable stock,
    made with 1 teaspoon
    Marigold bouillon powder
1 small green pepper, chopped
3 tablespoons tamari
175ml coconut milk
Grated zest and juice of 1 lime
50g French beans, chopped
Honey
Pepper
1 tablespoon basil leaves

Preheat the grill on a medium setting.

Toss the pumpkin in 1 tablespoon of the oil and grill until golden and soft, turning once, about 15 minutes.

Meanwhile, heat the remaining oil in a large saucepan and gently fry the shallots, garlic, dried and fresh chillies until soft, about 10 minutes.

Meanwhile, dry-roast the coriander and cumin seeds in a small frying pan. Tip into a mortar and pound to a powder with the pestle. Set aside. Using the same pan, dry-roast the peanuts. Pound until fine using the pestle and mortar.

Blend the lemongrass, ginger and Kaffir lime leaves into a purée with the water in a mini blender/chopper.

To the fried shallots and garlic, add the crushed coriander and cumin seeds, together with the lemongrass purée. Stir in well and cook, still stirring, for 1 minute.

Finally add the hot stock, roasted pumpkin cubes, green pepper, tamari, coconut milk, peanuts, lime zest and French beans. Bring to the boil and simmer until the French beans are al dente.

Season with the lime juice and honey and pepper to taste. Serve hot, scattering basil leaves over each bowlful.

LIGHT
BITES

moroccan carrots

Carrot and cinnamon make an excellent combination. This delicious salad provides a good contrast, and works well, with Red Pepper Purée (see opposite page), Baba Ghanoush (see page 41) and also Broad Bean Bissara (see page 42), when they are served as a group of salads for lunch or as a starter for a Moroccan feast.

SERVES 4–6

4 tablespoons olive oil
400g carrots, grated
2 garlic cloves, chopped
1 teaspoon ground cinnamon
4 tablespoons lemon juice
Salt

Heat the olive oil in a medium-sized saucepan over a moderate heat and sauté the carrots and garlic until they are soft but not coloured, about 10 minutes. Add the cinnamon, lemon juice and salt and cook gently for another 5 minutes.

Transfer to a bowl and leave at room temperature to cool. Serve the carrots cold.

VARIATION

Serve with 200g thick Greek yogurt on top of the carrots.

red pepper purée

Richly red *salada de felfla* is a favourite Moroccan starter or *kemia*, in which spiced vegetable purées are typically served alongside pickles and shiny green, purple and black olives. The myriad colours enchant both the eye and the palate. These glorious salads commonly remain on the table to serve as side dishes for the main course.

Serve this vibrant purée with carrot sticks or a selection of Crudités for Dipping (see pages 104–5).

SERVES 6

6 red Romano peppers
2 garlic cloves, chopped
Juice of 2 lemons
1 green chilli, deseeded and roughly chopped
1 teaspoon ground cumin
4 tablespoons olive oil
Salt
2 tablespoons chopped parsley
2 tablespoons chopped coriander

Grill the peppers and remove their skins (see page 177). Blend the peppers and their juices, along with the garlic, lemon juice, chilli, cumin and olive oil in a food processor. Season with salt.

Mix in the parsley and coriander and serve.

VARIATION

Add the chopped rind of half a preserved lemon.

ezme

This favourite Turkish *meze* of sunny red peppers and tomatoes with a hint of chilli comes in many variations – more or less spicy, and with the ingredients very finely chopped or blended to a paste (*ezme* is Turkish for 'crushed'). You could roast the peppers and even add a teaspoon of honey to the dressing for a sweet-sour effect. Be creative!

SERVES 6

2 red peppers
500g tomatoes
4 shallots or 1 red onion
4 garlic cloves
2 green chillies
Handful of parsley, leaves picked
4 sprigs of mint, leaves picked
Juice of 2 lemons
2 tablespoons tomato purée
4 tablespoons olive oil
Salt and pepper

Chop the peppers, tomatoes, shallots, garlic, chillies, parsley and mint as finely as you can, catching any juice, and mix together in a bowl.

In a second small bowl, combine the lemon juice, tomato purée and olive oil. Pour over the salad and season. Leave in the fridge for at least 1 hour to allow the flavours to develop.

VARIATIONS

– Add half a cucumber, finely diced.
– Sprinkle the salad with 30g toasted walnuts.

middle eastern
mezze

Just an hour to give friends a quick bite between work
and cycling off together to a concert or the cinema. Here is
an unusual and colourful array of *mezze* to delight and
sustain, which leaves everyone feeling alert for the evening's
entertainment. Arrange the food in the centre of the table
so that everyone can enjoy helping themselves to what
tempts them the most. Finish the pre-show bite with
syrupy Kibrizli Cake flavoured with lemon, honey and
sesame seeds, and serve it with a glass of hot tea
made with fresh mint from the garden.

SERVES 8–10

Falafel with Tahini Cream *pages 46–47*

Moroccan Carrots with greek yogurt *page 36*

Red Pepper Purée *page 37*

Ful Medames *page 45*

Avocado and Orange Salad
garnished with olives *page 153*

Red Cabbage and Roasted
Sunflower Seed Salad *page 159*

Kibrizli Cake with fresh mint tea *page 235*

TO DRINK

A medium-bodied fruity Spanish Rioja
accompanied by refreshing Belu sparkling water

baba ghanoush

Aubergines are the commonest vegetable in medieval Arab cookery books. They are also the one edible member of the deadly nightshade family (*Solancacea*) which originates in the Old World: India to be precise. The Arabs introduced aubergines to Spain alongside a wealth of wonderful foods – artichokes, carrots, spinach, bitter oranges, melons, dates, quinces, almonds and saffron – around the tenth century; whilst it was the Venetians who made them known to the Italians, through their trading with the Arabs.

Delectable, smoky *baba ghanoush* is ubiquitous throughout the Levant in many variations. Here, the richness of the aubergine is subtly balanced by the citrusy tang of the lemon with its zest. Serve it with carrot sticks or a selection of Crudités for Dipping (see pages 104–5).

SERVES 4–6

2 large aubergines
2 garlic cloves, chopped
2 tablespoons light tahini
Grated zest and juice of 1 lemon
3 tablespoons olive oil
Salt and pepper
2 tablespoons finely chopped parsley

Grill the aubergine (see page 177). Scoop out the flesh and combine it in a food processor with the garlic, tahini, zest and juice of the lemon and olive oil. Season.

Transfer to a bowl, scatter the parsley on top and serve.

VARIATIONS

– Garnish the finished purée with 100g pomegranate seeds and also 45g toasted pistachio nuts.
– Garnish the finished purée with 200g chopped cucumber, 150g halved cherry tomatoes, a chopped red Romano pepper and a finely chopped small red onion.
– Add 1 teaspoon cumin seeds to the food processor bowl when you combine the aubergine flesh with the garlic and tahini.

broad bean bissara

Beans are a Middle Eastern favourite for purées. Using frozen broad beans, *bissara* is wonderfully quick to make and useful to have at hand for surprise guests. Serve with carrot sticks or a selection of Crudités for Dipping (see pages 104–5).

SERVES 6

500g frozen broad beans
2 garlic cloves, roughly chopped
90ml olive oil, plus 1 tablespoon to garnish
2 tablespoons lemon juice
1 green chilli, chopped
1 teaspoon cumin seeds
1 teaspoon sweet paprika
Handful of coriander, leaves picked and roughly chopped,
    reserving a few leaves for garnish

Boil the broad beans until tender, about 5 minutes. Drain.

Transfer the broad beans to the food processor bowl, add the remaining ingredients, except the garnish, and blend. Serve garnished with a swirl of olive oil and some coriander leaves.

hummus

The word 'hummus' means 'chickpeas' in Arabic. Chickpeas were first cultivated in the Levant and Egypt and the earliest evidence of this dish dates from around 8000 BC. It is easy to see why it continues to appeal. Irresistible hummus can find a place at any meal. Serve this dish with sticks of raw carrot or celery.

SERVES 6

250g chickpeas
3 garlic cloves, roughly chopped
90ml lemon juice
2 teaspoons ground cumin
50ml olive oil
Salt

GARNISH SUGGESTIONS

Handful of chickpeas
2 tablespoons olive oil
1 teaspoon sweet paprika
1 tablespoon finely chopped parsley
1 tablespoon toasted pine nuts
2 tablespoons raisins

Cover the chickpeas generously with boiling water and soak overnight. Drain and rinse, then boil them in fresh water until totally soft, usually about 1 hour (but it depends on the age of the chickpeas). Drain thoroughly, reserving some of the cooking water.

Reserving a few chickpeas for garnish, put the rest into a food processor and add the garlic, lemon juice, cumin and olive oil with enough of the cooking water to blend the mixture into a soft cream. Add salt to taste.

Transfer the hummus to a plate and drizzle olive oil over it. Garnish with the reserved chickpeas, olive oil, paprika and parsley, or your chosen garnishes.

VARIATIONS

— Add 70g Slow-roasted Tomatoes (see page 260) and a handful of chopped parsley when blending, leaving out the cumin.
— Make *Hummus bi Tahina*, substituting 4 tablespoons light tahini for the olive oil and cumin.

ful medames

Ful medames is the Egyptian national dish; indeed, we know, through DNA tests on Egyptian mummies, that the pharaohs ate *ful medames* over three millennia ago. It is delicious, highly nutritious and a favourite breakfast dish, including for the evening break-fast of Ramadan. It can be eaten as a main meal with hard-boiled eggs on top and is often accompanied by olives, salad and pickled vegetables. It also makes an excellent *mezze*. Small dried fava beans can be found in Middle Eastern shops.

SERVES 6

250g *ful medames* (fava beans), soaked overnight
4 tablespoons olive oil
¼ teaspoon cumin seeds
Salt and pepper
4 eggs
3 ripe tomatoes, chopped
1 red oak leaf lettuce heart
3 spring onions, chopped
18 olives
2 tablespoons chopped parsley
1 lemon, quartered

Drain the soaked beans and put them in a large saucepan of fresh water. Boil until tender, about 45 minutes. Drain.

Heat the olive oil in a large saucepan over a medium-high heat. Add the cumin seeds and fry until they splutter and release their flavour.

Reduce the heat to low. Add the beans and heat through, about 8 minutes. Season with salt and pepper.

Meanwhile, boil the eggs for 8 minutes. Immediately cool them by running them under cold water. Shell, then cut vertically into quarters.

Serve the *ful medames* warm and decorated with eggs, tomatoes, lettuce leaves, spring onions and olives, with some parsley scattered on top and quarters of lemon.

VARIATION

Add a little chopped preserved lemon with the eggs, tomatoes and lettuce leaves.

falafel

Falafel is an ancient Middle Eastern dish made with dried white broad beans in Egypt. The Copts serve it especially during Lent, when meat is forbidden. Here, I have used chickpeas, as they do further east in Jordan, Lebanon and Syria. Falafel is typically served with tahini, a wide variety of colourful salads and perhaps some hummus (see page 43). *Nota bene*: this recipe uses dried chickpeas which are soaked and then ground; tinned chickpeas are already cooked and are thus unsuitable.

The great secret of this recipe is not to let the falafel mixture get too wet, so resist the temptation to put in a larger onion or extra herbs, which will result in a soggy mixture that will not hold together to form the falafel. To the same end, see that the chickpeas are thoroughly dry after they have been soaked, before grinding them in a food processor. If, like me, you are a falafel fanatic, it saves a great deal of time and effort to procure a falafel tool, which neatly presses out beautifully formed falafel shapes. These are easily found online.

Serve these falafel with Tahini Cream (see opposite page) and Red Cabbage and Roasted Sunflower Seed Salad (see page 159) – you could make these whilst the falafel mixture is chilling in the fridge.

SERVES 8

500g dried chickpeas
1 small red onion, roughly chopped
2 garlic cloves, roughly chopped
2 long, thin green chillies
6 tablespoons chopped coriander or parsley
2 teaspoons ground coriander
2 teaspoons ground cumin
¼ teaspoon bicarbonate of soda
½ teaspoon cream of tartar
Salt
Sunflower oil, for deep-frying

Soak the chickpeas in enough boiling water to cover them well and leave overnight or for at least 6 hours. Drain in a colander and rinse under the tap. Dry the chickpeas thoroughly on a tea towel.

Pulverise the chickpeas in a food processor. Add the other ingredients and blend thoroughly to a smooth paste. Season with salt. Shallow-fry a trial falafel and check that there is enough salt to bring out the flavour. Chill the remaining mixture for half an hour in the fridge.

Fill a deep-fat fryer two-thirds full with sunflower oil and heat the oil on a high setting. It has reached the appropriate heat, about 180°C, when it bubbles up around a trial falafel. Meanwhile, heat the oven to 100°C to keep the cooked falafel hot.

While the oil is heating, form the paste into walnut-sized balls, using a spoon or, better still, a falafel tool to assist you. Fill the chip basket with a layer of falafel without letting them touch one another. Lower them into the hot oil and fry until they are a rich, golden brown, about 2 minutes. If the oil bubbles up furiously when you put the falafel in, reduce the heat. Place the cooked falafel in the warm oven in a dish lined with kitchen paper in order to drain off the oil.

VARIATION

– For extra crunch, roll the falafel in sesame seeds immediately after you have shaped them, just before they are deep-fried.

tahini cream

This Arab starter is very popular in the Middle East. I love it with Falafel (see opposite page). You can also serve it with Crudités for Dipping (see pages 104–5).

SERVES 8

3 garlic cloves, roughly chopped
150ml lemon juice
150ml tahini
1 teaspoon ground cumin
75ml water
Salt and pepper
Chopped parsley, to garnish

Blend the garlic, lemon, tahini and cumin in a food processor. Add enough of the water to allow the mixture to form the consistency of single cream. Taste to see that the balance between the ingredients is correct, adjusting as necessary, and season.

Transfer to a bowl and garnish with parsley to serve.

persian toasted nuts

Tangy lime-toasted Persian nuts make fabulous nibbles alongside olives. We were introduced to them when the mother of our Iranian student Aydin tucked some into his suitcase for us, along with outstandingly perfumed Iranian saffron. Toasted nuts are one of the delicacies produced for the Iranian New Year, *Nowruz*, which is celebrated at the spring equinox. Iranians also use the same roasting technique for sunflower or pumpkin seeds. A fan oven is ideal for the final drying process.

SERVES 12 AS A SNACK

500g almonds
1 tablespoon sea salt
4 tablespoons boiling water
Juice of 3 limes

Heat the oven to 100°C.

Put the almonds into a stainless-steel frying pan over a high heat and stir constantly with a stainless steel spoon. Watch the almonds carefully – when they develop small, evenly spread, medium-brown spots, they are ready for the salt.

Dissolve the salt in the boiling water. Reduce the heat under the nuts and carefully pour the salty water over them. There will be lots of steam. Raise the heat again and keep stirring the nuts until they are dry. Then reduce the heat once more and add the lime juice. Once again, increase the heat and continue to stir the nuts until they are largely dry.

Put the nuts onto an oven tray and finish the drying process in the oven for 10 minutes.

VARIATION

Substitute sunflower or pumpkin seeds for the almonds.

indian chickpea flour pancakes

Indian *chilla* make both a delicious light supper and a fine brunch. They are typically eaten with chutneys, such as Cucumber Raita (see page 145), Cooked Green Mango Chutney (see page 268), Raw Green Mango Chutney (see page 269) or Quick Tomato Chutney (see page 269). They can also be served as the 'bread' with an Indian meal.

SERVES 3–4

170g chickpea flour
240ml water
3 garlic cloves, finely chopped
2cm piece of ginger root, grated
3 green chillies, deseeded and finely chopped
2 tablespoons finely chopped coriander
1 teaspoon turmeric
½ teaspoon fennel seeds
60ml lemon juice
1 teaspoon runny honey
½ teaspoon salt
4 tablespoons olive or sunflower oil, for frying
50g carrot, grated
50g courgette, grated

Put the chickpea flour in a bowl, add the water and blitz with a hand-held blender. Stir the garlic, ginger, chillies, fresh coriander, turmeric and fennel seeds into the batter. Season with the lemon juice, honey and salt. Leave the batter to rest for 15 minutes.

Put the oil into a ramekin and have a pastry brush, a teaspoon and a small measuring cup to hand. Place a small 20cm non-stick frying pan (which has a lid) on a low to medium heat. Smear the pan with 1 teaspoon of oil and tilt the pan to cover it in the oil. Add the carrot and courgette to the batter and stir well. Pour about 90ml of the batter into the pan and tilt the pan to spread the batter to the edges, using a spoon to encourage it if necessary. Cover and cook until the underside of the pancake is reddish brown and the top is set, about 3 minutes. Brush the top of the pancake lightly with oil and turn it over. Cook the second side, uncovered, until golden, about 1½ minutes.

Remove the pancake from the pan and ideally serve it immediately, or put it on a plate in the oven to keep it warm and repeat with the rest of the batter (remember to stir it well each time before use) and serve all the pancakes together. This quantity of batter makes 8–10 pancakes.

farinata

Cooked in a searing wood-burning oven, crispy Italian chickpea flour *farinata* is a favourite street snack in Liguria and Tuscany. You can eat it with marinated artichoke hearts and juicy olives as a starter and it makes a great brunch with salad and cheese. Indeed, you can melt some Taleggio slices on top during the last five minutes of the cooking time, or serve two small ones with a thick slice of grilled aubergine marinated in garlic and chilli sandwiched between them. If you are fortunate enough to be able to cook *farinata* in a wood-burning oven, they cook in minutes as you watch them.

Resting the batter allows it to start fermenting, which lightens the texture. However if you can only leave it for 20 minutes it is still mouth-wateringly delicious.

SERVES 6

250g chickpea flour
750ml water
75ml olive oil, plus 2 tablespoons for cooking
2 teaspoons Maldon sea salt
Pepper
2 sprigs of rosemary, leaves picked

Put the chickpea flour, water and olive oil into a large bowl and blend with a hand-held blender. Ideally, let the batter rest at room temperature for 2 hours or even overnight.

Preheat the oven to 220°C.

With a slotted spoon, remove any foam that has formed at the top of the batter. Stir 1 teaspoon of the salt and some pepper into the batter. Put 2 tablespoons oil into a 30 × 34cm baking tin and pour in the batter (it should be about 5mm deep). Cook for 10 minutes, then sprinkle the remaining salt and the rosemary leaves over the top, which will have started to develop a skin and become golden. Return to the oven and cook until the *farinata* is crispy brown and firm to the touch, about a further 10 minutes. Serve immediately.

VARIATION

Using a mandoline, slice 4 small artichokes and substitute them for the rosemary and salt. Put them in a small bowl of water with the juice of 1 lemon as you slice them to prevent them from going brown. When you have finished slicing, drain and dress them in olive oil with salt and pepper. Place on the *farinata* for the second half of the cooking.

courgette flowers with sage leaves

There's nothing like going into the garden, choosing your courgette flowers and sage leaves, frying them in a meltingly light batter in a generous amount of olive oil and eating them immediately *al fresco* in the sun. What joy!

Traditionally, bunches of male flowers are sold in French and Italian markets, but female flowers with a perfectly formed miniature courgette attached look enchanting. For Sunday brunch, stuff your courgette flowers, or *fiori di zucchini*, with goats' cream cheese, lemon zest and tarragon or thyme before lowering them into the batter.

SERVES 6

200g chickpea flour
220ml water
40g Parmesan cheese, grated
Salt and pepper
Olive oil, for shallow-frying
12 courgette flowers
18 sage leaves with their stalks

Mix the chickpea flour with enough of the water to make a batter with the consistency of yogurt. Add the Parmesan and season.

Heat 4 tablespoons olive oil in a frying pan. Holding onto their stalks, dip the courgette flowers and sage leaves into the batter and shallow-fry them in batches, turning them once, until golden on both sides, about 5 minutes. You will probably need to add more oil for subsequent batches. Keep the cooked courgette flowers and sage leaves warm in an oven set to 100°C until all the batches are cooked. Serve immediately.

champignons à la grecque

The French phrase *à la* plus a name became a popular shorthand to indicate the preparation of specific dishes in late nineteenth- and early twentieth-century France. Indeed, the coding became so complicated that lexicons, which gourmets would tuck into their coat pockets, were produced to explain the meanings.

A dish prepared *à la grecque* (in the Greek manner) uses olive oil and lemon juice with herbs and spices – a technique applied to a wide range of fresh, young vegetables such as artichokes and fennel. In this case, mushrooms, they absorb the flavour of the crushed coriander, bay leaves and lemon deliciously.

SERVES 4–6

6 tablespoons olive oil
2 teaspoons coriander seeds, crushed
500g white button mushrooms, trimmed
   and halved
3 bay leaves
Juice of 1 lemon
Salt and pepper

Heat 4 tablespoons of the oil in a frying pan (which has a lid) and gently roast the crushed coriander seeds until fragrant. Add the mushrooms, bay leaves and half the lemon juice and continue to sauté over a low heat for 1 minute. Cover the pan and leave them to cook gently for a further 4 minutes.

Transfer the mushrooms, with their juices and the bay leaves, to a serving dish. Season. Sprinkle with the remaining olive oil and lemon juice. Serve warm or cold.

tortilla

Frying potatoes and onions in lots of deep green extra virgin olive oil, as recommended by my son Alex, gives this tortilla an irresistible flavour. (Keep the leftover oil for subsequent frying.) It is essential, too, to choose beautiful waxy potatoes such as Charlotte, Desirée or my favourites, Chérie and the wonderfully flavoured, knobbly nineteenth-century Pink Fir Apples.

This tortilla makes a superb canapé: cut it into diamonds or squares and serve either with a blob of Aïoli (see page 256) on each diamond, with a slow-roasted tomato (see page 260) perched on top in summer, or an olive in winter. Leave the omelette to cool completely before cutting it, so that it holds together.

SERVES 3–4 (OR 12 AS A CANAPÉ)

350ml olive oil
2 onions, finely sliced
6 eggs
Salt and pepper
600g waxy potatoes, finely sliced

In a large frying pan, heat the olive oil over a low heat and gently fry the onions until soft, about 15 minutes.

Meanwhile, beat the eggs in a medium bowl and season.

Drain the onions in a sieve, holding back the oil. When the onions have cooled slightly, add them to the eggs.

Pour the drained oil back into the frying pan. Fry half the potatoes until cooked, turning them over once, about 10 minutes. Drain the potatoes in the sieve, holding back the oil, and add them to the eggs. Use the saved oil for cooking the second batch of potatoes and repeat the process. Once again, reserve the oil after cooking the potatoes.

Take a 20cm frying pan, pour in 3 tablespoons of the reserved oil and heat until hot. Add the egg and potato mixture, which should nearly fill the pan, reduce the heat to medium-low and cook until the tortilla begins to come away from the edge of the pan and is almost set, about 10 minutes. Check it is freed from the edge with a spatula. Take a large plate or flat frying pan lid, of a diameter that is larger than the frying pan, place it over the pan and invert the pan so that the tortilla falls onto the plate. Add 1 tablespoon oil to the pan and gently slide the tortilla back into it with the browned side facing upwards. Cook until just set, about 5 minutes. Slide the tortilla out onto a plate and serve.

late and lazy sunday brunch

Typically for young professionals, my kids relish brunch at the weekend, perhaps enhanced by wonderful cheeses from their local Italian delicatessen. Often they have friends round to join them in the tiny garden (complete with home-made wood-burning oven) of their ex-council house flat before going out for a good walk along the Regent's canal. The atmosphere is relaxed and the array of dishes, eclectic, with everyone mucking in and cooking whatever takes their fancy, taking inspiration from their deli foraging, what looks good in the garden and an intrepid rummage in the fridge. This menu aims to capture their eclecticism and fun.

SERVES 8–10

Avocado and Poached Eggs *opposite page*

Farinata *page 50*

Courgette and Spinach Fritters *page 80*

Cauliflower and Caper Salad *page 160*

Swiss Carrot Cake *page 234*

EASY ADDITIONS

Roast peppers and artichokes, and a couple of interesting cheeses *from the local deli*

TO DRINK

Fruit juices, tea and coffee, and a crisp white Burgundy such as Saint-Verain

avocado and poached eggs

Poached eggs are a common feature of the kids' brunches. They can be perched on top of lentils, vegetables and salads. The secret of success is truly fresh eggs, whose circle of white holds together perfectly around a plump yolk. Water that is just boiling when the eggs go in helps to give them a rounded shape. The cooking time also depends on the freshness of the egg: eggs straight from the hen take slightly longer to cook.

This recipe from my kids is a perennial favourite.

SERVES 4

2 avocados
3 tablespoons olive oil
Salt and pepper
60g rocket
4 eggs
2 tablespoons white wine vinegar

Using a fork, roughly mash the avocados with 2 tablespoons of the olive oil. Season.

Lightly mix the rocket with the remaining olive oil. Season.

Divide the mashed avocado between 4 small plates, making a little dent in the middle of each mound, ready for the egg. Lay a quarter of the rocket on each plate beside the avocado.

Break each egg into a ramekin or cup. Fill a large saucepan one-third full of boiling water from the kettle, add the wine vinegar and bring just to the boil. Gently slip each egg into the water, lightly shaping it with a slotted spoon if necessary. Once they are all in, reduce the heat so the water just simmers. A soft fresh egg will take about 3 minutes. You can inspect it with a slotted spoon and give it a bit longer if needed.

Lift the poached egg out of the cooking water with the slotted spoon, giving it a little shake to release any water. Place the poached egg on the mashed avocado and serve.

VARIATIONS

– Sprinkle a small pinch of hot sweet paprika on each egg.
– Drizzle 1–2 teaspoons pesto over each egg.

grilled avocado with roquefort and walnuts

A delicious and dead-easy starter using Roquefort. The Roquefort caves at the edge of the spectacular and wildly romantic Gorges du Tarn – which remain between 7°C and 9°C at 95 per cent humidity, day and night throughout the year – offer the perfect conditions for maturing Roquefort. The cheese, made from local ewes' milk, is inoculated with *Penicillium roqueforti*, which is found in the soil of the caves. Roquefort was the first recipient of France's *Appellation d'Origine* in 1925.

When combining the Roquefort and walnuts, leave the chunks of nut quite large.

SERVES 4

125g Roquefort cheese
125g walnuts
2 avocados

Preheat the grill on a medium setting.

In a food processor, roughly combine the Roquefort and walnuts.

Chop the avocados in half and remove the stone. Fill the resulting hole with the Roquefort-and-nut mixture and cover the tops of the avocados with the mixture as well.

Grill the avocados for about 1 minute until golden, taking care not to burn the nuts. Serve immediately.

VARIATION

Substitute cashews for the walnuts, and halloumi for the Roquefort.

grilled beetroot with asparagus and halloumi

Succulent young beetroots are ideal for this dish, but mature beetroots make a fine alternative. In the latter case, first cook the beetroot with a little water in the microwave on a high setting for about 15 minutes, or bake in the oven as for Baked Beetroot (see page 179). Peel and dice the cooked beetroot. When asparagus is out of season, purple sprouting broccoli or French beans make good alternatives.

We are fortunate in getting wonderful Welsh artisan goats' halloumi in Cardiff farmers' market, which makes this dish a family favourite.

SERVES 6

250g asparagus
1kg baby beetroots, chopped into quarters
4 tablespoons olive oil
1 teaspoon cumin seeds
400g halloumi, chopped into 1.5cm cubes
30g butter
30ml balsamic vinegar
Handful of chopped parsley

Preheat the grill on a medium-high setting.

Trim any tough bases off the asparagus spears and blanch them in boiling water for 30 seconds to 1 minute, depending on their thickness. Remove, plunge into icy water and pat dry with a tea towel.

Put the beetroots and blanched asparagus on a grill pan, drizzle with 2 tablespoons of the olive oil and sprinkle with the cumin seeds. Grill, turning from time to time, until the beetroots are soft and wrinkly and the asparagus is slighly charred, 5–10 minutes.

Meanwhile, toss the halloumi cubes in 1 tablespoon olive oil and fry on a hot griddle pan, turning them from time to time, until golden, about 5 minutes. Mix the halloumi with the beetroot and asparagus.

Heat the butter and balsamic vinegar in a saucepan over a low heat.

Divide the beetroot, asparagus and halloumi between 6 individual plates. Pour over the balsamic vinegar and butter mixture, scatter over the chopped parsley and serve.

VARIATION

Serve on a bed of rocket.

charcoal-grilled asparagus
with romesco sauce

Romesco is a nutty Catalan sauce, eaten with *calçots*, succulent spring onions. In February, when *calçots* come into season, the Catalans hold open-air *calçotades*, when *calçots* are roasted over open fires until their outer layer is charred. The charred layer is removed and the tender insides are dipped into the *salsa de romesco*. Slim leeks make an excellent substitute for *calçots* but grilled asparagus is also delicious.

SERVES 4

16 asparagus spears
30g flaked almonds (optional)

ROMESCO SAUCE

100g blanched almonds
50g shelled hazelnuts
3 Romano peppers
5 tablespoons olive oil
3 garlic cloves, roughly
    chopped

1 small dried red chilli,
    deseeded and crumbled
½ teaspoon sweet smoked
    paprika
1 teaspoon tomato purée
1 tablespoon sherry vinegar or
    lemon juice
Salt and pepper

Preheat the oven to 180°C. Preheat the grill on a medium-high setting.

To make the sauce, roast the nuts in the oven for 8 minutes.

Grill the peppers and remove their skins (see page 177). When they are ready, reduce the grill setting to medium, ready for the asparagus.

Meanwhile, heat 1 tablespoon of the oil in a pan over a low heat and gently fry the garlic until it is golden, about 8 minutes.

Blend the nuts, peppers, garlic, chilli, paprika, tomato purée and the remaining oil to a paste in a food processor. Add the vinegar. Season.

Blanch the asparagus in boiling water for 30 seconds to 1 minute, depending on its thickness. Plunge it into icy water and pat dry.

Dry-roast the flaked almonds in a pan until golden, 2–3 minutes.

Grill the asparagus, turning it once, until soft and slightly charred, about 5 minutes. Serve the asparagus with a dollop of *romesco*, sprinkled with flaked almonds, if using.

VARIATION

Substitute 1cm slices of fennel or sliced baby artichokes for the asparagus. Blanch for 45 seconds and continue as above.

choufleur forqueray

After finishing my PhD I visited the descendant of the Forquerays, who were formidable players of the viola da gamba during the reigns of Louis XIV and XV, on whom I'd written my thesis. He welcomed me with open arms and feasted me on this recipe – his response to my grain-free vegetarian requirements – in the dining room of his 32-bedroom chateau in the Haute Loire, which he and his wife looked after single handedly. After lunch he proudly showed me his excellent vegetable garden, situated close to the house, from whence the superb cauliflower and amazingly flavoursome tomatoes had come. The hens, whose eggs had gone into the mayonnaise, were scratching around merrily in their idyllic surroundings. His wife took me down to the vast cellars where I was given a lesson in making the goats' cheese we had also eaten for lunch. She gave me one of her little plastic colanders to have a try myself, warning me not to make this cheese during a thunderstorm as it would curdle. I was then introduced to the local farmer and his wife, who had sheltered a British pilot for 18 months during the Second World War, hiding him in their cellar and escorting him up for fresh air in the depths of the night. A memorable day!

The perfect conditions in which the cauliflower and tomatoes were grown, combined with their absolute freshness, transformed a simple dish into a feast.

SERVES 6

1 large cauliflower
200ml mayonnaise (see page 256)
4 tomatoes, quartered
2 tablespoons chopped parsley

Remove the green leaves from the cauliflower and, with a sharp knife, cut a deep 'X' into the base of the stem. Steam the cauliflower, whole, until just cooked, 10–15 minutes. (Meanwhile, make the mayonnaise.)

When the cauliflower is ready, place it in a serving dish and leave it to cool. When it is warm rather than hot, pour the mayonnaise over it. Decorate with the tomatoes, sprinkle with parsley and serve.

VARIATION

Use Aïoli (see page 256) instead of the mayonnaise.

olive pâté

This dark, rich pâté is a winner for canapés. It is beautifully complemented by tangy Blini (see page 102), garnished with soured cream and a little parsley; but it is equally good elegantly perched on a small leaf of chicory or Little Gem lettuce. Good-quality Kalamata olives make a fine choice for this recipe. Serve this pâté with carrot sticks.

SERVES 4–6

1 tablespoon olive oil
6 spring onions, finely chopped (use up to 4cm of the green parts)
2 garlic cloves, finely chopped
6 tomatoes, skinned and chopped
125g stoned purple or black olives, pulverised in a food processor
½ teaspoon fennel seeds
1 tablespoon honey
175ml red wine
Chopped parsley, to garnish

Heat the olive oil in a large pan over a low heat and soften the spring onions and garlic, about 10 minutes. Stir in the tomatoes, olives, fennel seeds and honey and cook gently for 10 minutes.

Add the red wine and bring to the boil. Reduce the heat and simmer, uncovered, for 20 minutes. Increase the heat and reduce to create a soft pâté. Leave to cool.

Serve in a brightly coloured pottery bowl garnished with a little chopped parsley.

globe artichokes with aïoli

Artichokes, cultivated thistles, are grown all around the Mediterranean and were enjoyed by the ancient Greeks and Romans. Their name is a corruption of the Arabic *al'qarshuf*, and they are members of the lettuce family. Artichokes are easy to grow – save that slugs are partial to the young leaves – and their pointed grey-green foliage looks splendidly majestic in the garden; if you miss the edible artichoke bud it transforms into a wonderful deep indigo flower which attracts bees and other beneficial insects.

Once the globe is served, pick off each leaf separately and dip it into the aïoli before eating the fleshy base of the leaf. When you finally get to the centre, scrape or cut off the inedible hairy 'choke' and eat the succulent heart – the best part – spread liberally with the aïoli. As Alan Davidson points out in the *Oxford Companion to Food*, the patience required to eat the artichoke, well rewarded by its luscious nutty taste, gives rise in Italy to the saying *la politica del carciofo* which translates as 'the politics of dealing with your opponents one by one' (*carciofo* means 'artichoke'). Voltaire describes the joy of eating his own fresh artichokes in winter and the sixteenth-century French poet Pierre de Ronsard declared that artichokes are better than the finest meats. He wrote lyrically about eating them while being stretched out beside a stream and listening to the sound of water.

SERVES 6

6 globe artichokes
250ml Aïoli (see page 256)

Boil the artichokes until they are cooked – the cooking time can vary from 15–40 minutes depending on the size of the globe. The artichokes are cooked when a leaf comes away easily from the base of the globe. You can make the aïoli while the artichokes are cooking.

Drain the hot artichokes thoroughly and serve immediately with the bowl of aïoli.

VARIATION

Serve with melted butter, Hollandaise Sauce (see page 257) or Vinaigrette made with pomegranate molasses (see page 259).

vignole

This Italian stew is full of the joys of spring. The taste is most intense with fresh broad beans and peas, but frozen ones can be substituted. For the best aesthetic results, blanch the broad beans for one minute, then peel them to reveal their shiny green insides before adding them to the frying pan with the peas and lemon zest.

SERVES 4–5

Grated zest and juice of 1 lemon
6 baby artichokes, 100g each (before trimming)
5 tablespoons olive oil
3 shallots, chopped
4 garlic cloves, finely chopped
100g tomatoes, chopped
300g podded broad beans
300g shelled peas
Up to 75ml stock, made with ¼ teaspoon Marigold buillon powder
Up to 75ml white wine
Salt and pepper
Handful of mint leaves
Handful of basil leaves

Set aside 1 tablespoon of the lemon juice and put the remaining juice in a bowl of water, ready for the sliced artichokes.

Preparing 1 artichoke at a time, pull off the tough outer leaves to reveal the younger pale green leaves underneath. Chop off the spiky artichoke top and, using a potato peeler, pare the fibrous skin off the stem. Trim the stem to neaten. Slice the artichoke and immediately submerge it in the bowl of lemon juice and water.

In either a large frying pan (which has a lid) or a saucepan, heat 4 tablespoons of the olive oil over a low heat and gently sauté the shallots until they are soft, about 10 minutes. Add the garlic and sauté for another minute. Then add the artichoke slices and cook them until they start to colour, about 5 minutes. Add the chopped tomatoes and fry them with all the other ingredients until the tomatoes soften, about 5 minutes. Finally, add the broad beans, peas and lemon zest. Just cover the vegetables with the stock and white wine. Cover the pan and simmer over a low heat until the vegetables are soft, about 8 minutes. When the vegetables are soft, season and sprinkle with the reserved lemon juice to taste. Add the mint and basil leaves. Drizzle with the remaining olive oil to serve.

artichoke heart dip

Canned artichoke hearts are relatively successful, but you need to rinse off the brine thoroughly. The Spanish present artichoke hearts as a hot tapas, fried in rich green olive oil with sun-dried red chilli and garlic. You can marinate them in olive oil with herbs and garlic and serve them as a cold tapas. This American starter is speedy to make; keeping a couple of cans of artichokes in the larder gives you a tasty and unusual dish to hand. Serve with carrot sticks.

SERVES 6

2 × 400g cans artichoke hearts, drained
1 garlic clove, finely chopped
Grated zest of ½ lemon
200ml Mayonnaise (see page 256)
75g Parmesan cheese, grated
75g Manchego cheese, grated

Preheat the oven to 180°C (unless you wish to cook this dish in a microwave oven – see below).

Rinse the brine off the artichoke hearts in a colander and chop them in half vertically. Put them in a bowl.

Add the garlic and lemon zest to the mayonnaise. Mix in the cheeses.

Place the artichoke hearts in an ovenproof dish and heat them until hot, either in the preheated oven, about 5 minutes, or in a microwave oven on a high setting, about 2 minutes. Mix in the mayonnaise and serve immediately.

aubergine skorthalia

Aubergine *Skorthalia* is believed to be a very ancient dish; this
version, using potato rather than bread, probably came from the
Greek island of Cephalonia. My recipe is from Kalamaras, a
favourite Greek restaurant in Bayswater that we used to visit
for special occasions as a family when I was a teenager.

I love this recipe, but it is not for the fainthearted as far as
garlic is concerned: it is seriously garlicky.

SERVES 6–8

500g aubergines, sliced sideways into 1cm-thick rounds
1 small potato (45g), boiled until soft and peeled
100g ground almonds
4–5 garlic cloves, chopped
2½ tablespoons lemon juice
100ml olive oil, plus extra for brushing
Parsley leaves, chopped, to garnish

Preheat the grill on a medium setting.

Lightly oil a baking tray and place the aubergine slices on it. Brush
the upper sides generously with olive oil. Grill the aubergine rounds
until soft and golden, turning them once, about 8 minutes. Drain on
kitchen paper.

To make the *skorthalia*, blend the potato, ground almonds, garlic and
lemon juice to a paste in a food processor. Then, through the feeder,
add the olive oil very slowly with the motor running, as if making
mayonnaise, until the mixture is combined in a smooth emulsion.

Spread the *skorthalia* on the aubergine slices and serve garnished
with the parsley.

EVERYDAY
MAINS

oeufs florentine

Spinach originated in the Middle East and its name is derived from the Persian, *aspanākh*. Twelfth-century Arab writer Ibn al-Awam rated it the 'prince of vegetables' and seventeeth-century writer and gardener John Evelyn recommends boiling it 'in its own moisture', adding that it 'is a most excellent condiment with butter, vinegar, or limon'.

The French term 'Florentine' denotes the use of spinach in a dish, suggesting the influence of Florence on the French taste for spinach. France was deeply impressed by the achievements of the Medicis in the sixteenth century, including their knowledge of vegetable growing and cookery. The refreshing idea of a tomato slice under each half egg comes from a memorable family meal near Bergerac.

SERVES 6

9 eggs
1kg spinach, chopped
50g butter, plus extra for greasing
Salt and pepper
Nutmeg
3 tomatoes
1 quantity nutmeg-flavoured Béchamel Sauce (see
  page 258: nutmeg variation)
60g Manchego or Emmental cheese, grated

Preheat the oven to 170°C. Bring a pan of water to the boil.

Boil the eggs for 8 minutes. Drain the eggs and plunge them into icy water to stop them from cooking further. Shell them and cut each egg in half vertically.

While the eggs boil, wash the spinach thoroughly, give it a shake and place it in a saucepan with some water still clinging to the leaves. Put on a lid and steam over a medium heat until cooked, about 2 minutes. Drain. Mix in the butter and season with salt, pepper and a generous pinch of freshly grated nutmeg.

Butter a large gratin dish and place the spinach in the bottom. Cut the tomatoes into 1cm-thick slices. Place each egg half on 1 tomato slice and lay these on top of the spinach. Make the béchamel sauce and pour it over the eggs. Sprinkle the cheese on top. Bake until the cheese melts and the dish is heated through, about 15 minutes.

VARIATION

Substitute 400g crème fraîche for the béchamel sauce.

eggs with tomatoes and red peppers

Regional variations on this delicious and simple dish are found all round the Mediterranean. *Uova al pomodoro con peperoni* comes from Tuscany. If your tomatoes are not beautiful sweet Mediterranean ones, add a little honey when you season. This delicious dish makes the ultimate brunch.

SERVES 4–5

2 red peppers, halved vertically
2 yellow peppers, halved vertically
2 tablespoons olive oil
4 garlic cloves, chopped
750g large tomatoes, roughly chopped
Salt and pepper
8 small eggs
Handful of basil or parsley, leaves picked and chopped

Preheat the grill on a medium setting.

Grill the peppers until cooked, about 10 minutes, turning them once. Slice into 1.5cm ribbons.

While the peppers are grilling, heat the olive oil in a large frying pan (which has a lid) and lightly fry the garlic over a low heat. Add the tomatoes, increase the heat to medium-low and simmer until soft, about 15 minutes. Mix in the peppers and continue simmering until the sauce is reduced, about 5 minutes more. Season. (If the sauce becomes too dry, add a little water.)

Make 8 little hollows in the tomato-and-pepper mixture and break an egg into each hollow. Cover the pan and cook on a gentle heat until the eggs have set, about 10 minutes.

Serve hot sprinkled with basil or parsley.

VARIATIONS

— Add a handful of chopped black olives, 1 tablespoon capers and 1 teaspoon paprika or harissa to the tomato sauce with the peppers.
— Instead of poaching the eggs, make a large cavity in the middle of the tomato sauce and add a pool of beaten egg (made using 8 eggs). Gently stir the mixture until it sets.

mushroom and asparagus quiche

Quiches are excellent cold, on picnics, or as a delicious main dish to be taken to a friend's house and heated when you arrive. Fillings could be spinach, courgettes, or goats' cheese and watercress – all added to the oniony custard.

SERVES 8

1 quantity Quiche Crust (see
   page 277), seasoned with salt
4 tablespoons olive oil
2 large onions, chopped
3 garlic cloves, chopped
5 eggs
350ml cream
4 sprigs of lemon thyme,
   leaves picked

Salt and pepper
½ nutmeg, grated
500g chestnut mushrooms,
   trimmed
30g butter, plus extra
   for greasing
400g asparagus, trimmed
90g Emmental cheese, grated

Preheat the oven to 180°C.

Grease a 28cm quiche dish with the butter, then spread the quiche crust mixture over the base and sides. Bake until lightly browned and slightly crispy, about 10 minutes. Set aside.

Heat 2 tablespoons of the olive oil in a pan and fry the onions and garlic over a low heat until golden, about 15 minutes. Mix the eggs and cream in a large bowl. Add the fried onions and thyme leaves, then season with salt, pepper and the nutmeg. Set aside.

Slice any large mushrooms, but decent-sized chunks are good. Fry the mushrooms gently in a large frying pan in the remaining olive oil. Leave them to colour, then add the butter and stir the mushrooms around so that they absorb it. Add the mushrooms to the onions, eggs and cream.

Bring a pan of water to the boil. Cut any large asparagus spears in half. Blanch the asparagus for 1 minute.

Fill the potato base with the mushroom custard. Arrange the asparagus spears on top and sprinkle the Emmental across the top. Bake until the top is golden and the custard is set, about 25 minutes.

VARIATION

Make a spinach quiche by substituting 400g cooked spinach, roughly chopped, for the mushrooms and asparagus. Add to the onions, eggs and cream. Fill the potato base with the custard and continue as above.

chard soufflé

Soufflés are easy to make and always exciting. They work on the principle that air expands as it is heated up. The converse is also true, so a soufflé needs to be served as quickly as possible. You can either bake them quickly (220°C) for 15–20 minutes or slowly (180°C) for about 40 minutes. The fast ones are lighter but fall swiftly; slower-cooked soufflés are more stable. Soufflés made using a comparatively heavy base vegetable ingredient, such as chard, are better cooked slowly. The light texture of potato flour with its mild taste lends itself to soufflé making. I love the earthy and unconventional look of serving my soufflé in a Spanish terracotta dish.

SERVES 4

450g chard (or spinach)
60g butter, plus extra for
  greasing
30ml olive oil
2 tablespoons potato flour
300ml milk

Nutmeg
60g Manchego cheese, grated
5 eggs, separated
1 egg white
Salt and pepper

Preheat the oven to 180°C and butter a medium-sized (1 litre) soufflé dish or a high-sided ovenproof dish.

Wash the chard thoroughly and remove any tough stems. Dry it in a salad spinner and chop it up. Cook over a medium heat in 30g of the butter and the olive oil until soft.

Make a béchamel sauce with the remaining butter, the potato flour and milk (see page 258), adding a grating of nutmeg, to taste, to the milk at the start. Beat the egg yolks with an electric whisk in a large bowl. Lightly fold in the béchamel sauce, cheese and chard.

After cleaning the whisk beaters, beat the 6 egg whites in a large bowl until stiff. Lightly fold in the chard mixture with a large metal spoon. (Your soufflé can wait in the fridge for up to 4 hours at this point.)

Transfer the mixture carefully to the prepared baking dish. Bake until the soufflé has risen, is firm and the top has browned, about 40 minutes. Serve at once!

VARIATION

Substitute 450g finely chopped courgettes for the chard. When you add the cooked courgette to the egg mixture, add a handful of chopped flat-leaf parsley at the same time.

provençal courgette flan with tomato, olive and caper sauce

I love this sunny Provençal flan or *tian* of Claudia Roden's. It should be moist when it comes out of the oven and the courgettes should still have a hint of crunch. Use best-quality olives and capers in the sauce, which lifts the subtle custard. The word *tian* originally referred to the earthenware dish in which this recipe was made, but now embraces the flan itself. Vegetables with a high water content (spinach, mushrooms or tomatoes) are particularly suited to *tians*. So once my courgette plants are producing copious fruit, I look forward to this dish.

SERVES 4

2 onions, chopped
2 tablespoons olive oil
4 eggs
125ml milk
Salt and pepper
Nutmeg
500g courgettes, thinly sliced
Butter, for greasing

SAUCE

1 tablespoon olive oil
2 garlic cloves
500g tomatoes, chopped
Salt and pepper
1–2 tablespoons honey
2 tablespoons black olives,
    coarsely chopped
2 tablespoons capers, drained

Preheat the oven to 180°C. Thoroughly grease a 26cm-diameter ovenproof dish.

Fry the onion gently in the oil until soft, about 15 minutes.

In a medium-sized bowl, beat the eggs with a fork. Add the milk, season with salt, pepper and a grating of nutmeg to taste and beat some more. Add the fried onions and the courgettes. Mix together.

Transfer the mixture to the prepared dish and bake until firm, about 1½ hours. (Cover the dish with greaseproof paper for the first ½ hour, so that the top does not become over-brown.)

Meanwhile, cook the sauce. Heat the oil in a saucepan and gently fry the garlic until golden. Add the tomatoes and season, adjusting the amount of honey to compensate for any lack of sweetness in the tomatoes. Simmer until reduced, about 20 minutes. Add the olives and capers and cook for another 3 minutes.

Either serve the *tian* from its dish or turn it out onto a warm plate. Serve in slices, with the tomato sauce poured on top.

courgette and spinach fritters

Courgettes combine well with chickpea flour and, together, they make delicious fritters. The spinach, feta and lemon zest in this recipe lift the courgettes onto an exciting plane. There is probably enough salt in the feta for these fritters.

   These fritters can be served hot or cold, and they heat up well in the oven. Try them accompanied by a chutney (see pages 268–9) – I like to serve them with the Cooked Green Mango Chutney.

SERVES 4

Olive oil, for frying
6 spring onions, finely chopped
60g chickpea flour
4 eggs
3 tablespoons chopped coriander
1 red chilli, finely chopped
Grated zest of 1 lemon
75g feta cheese, grated
30g Parmesan cheese, grated
270g courgettes, grated
150g baby spinach, roughly chopped
Pepper

Heat 1 tablespoon olive oil in a small frying pan and cook the spring onions over a low heat until they are soft, about 8 minutes.

Using a hand-held blender, beat the chickpea flour and the eggs together in a bowl. Add the cooked spring onions, coriander, chilli, lemon zest, feta and Parmesan and stir. Then add the grated courgettes and stir again. Finally, stir in the spinach. Season with pepper.

Heat 1 tablespoon olive oil in a large frying pan (26cm) over a medium heat to fry the first batch of fritters. For fritters of about 7cm diameter that are 1cm thick, use 2 tablespoons batter per fritter, frying several at a time and shaping them into circles gently with a spoon. Turning each fritter once, cook until both sides are golden, about 2–3 minutes on the first side and 2 minutes on the second. Repeat with the remaining batter, using 1 tablespoon olive oil to fry each batch.

Place the fritters on an ovenproof dish and keep them warm in a low oven (at 100°C) until you are ready to eat them.

roast vegetables with pesto

Roast vegetables make a delicious supper throughout the year. To make them crispy, place the vegetables in a single layer on the roasting tray. Serve with a bowl of Pesto (see page 263) or Aïoli (see page 256).

SERVES 4–6

2 red onions, roughly chopped
1 aubergine, halved lengthways, chopped into chunks
2 red peppers, halved and sliced into wide ribbons
1 fennel bulb, sliced
2 waxy potatoes, cut into small pieces
4 baby carrots, cut vertically in half, leaving 4cm of stalk
6 whole garlic cloves, unpeeled
30g lemon, rind and flesh finely chopped
5 tablespoons olive oil
2 teaspoons coriander seeds, crushed
Salt
2 courgettes, halved and sliced into half moons
250g cherry tomatoes
200g mushrooms, trimmed
1 teaspoon black peppercorns, crushed
Handful of parsley, roughly chopped
Handful of coriander, roughly chopped

Preheat the oven to 210°C.

Put the onion, aubergine, peppers, fennel, potatoes, carrots, garlic and chopped lemon peel and flesh in a bowl and coat with 3 tablespoons of the oil. Add half the crushed coriander seeds, season with salt and toss well with your hands. Put the vegetables in a single layer on 1 large or 2 medium baking trays. Roast the vegetables for 15 minutes, then turn them. Continue to roast until nearly cooked, about 10 minutes.

Meanwhile, put the courgettes, cherry tomatoes and mushrooms in a bowl with the remaining oil and crushed coriander, the crushed pepper and a small pinch of salt. Mix well. Once the first batch of vegetables has cooked for 25 minutes, stir in these additions. Cook until brown and crispy, about 15 minutes. Serve scattered with the herbs.

VARIATION

Place thick slices of Taleggio or goats' cheese on top of the vegetables when you add the courgettes.

barbecue

Vegetables come into their own when grilled over hot coals or wood embers. I usually line the barbecue base with heavy-duty foil, both to reflect the heat and to keep it clean, and brush the grill with oil to stop the food sticking. Try potatoes, and sweet potatoes, wrapped in foil and cooked in the embers for about an hour – delicious! I did this as a child when my parents had a bonfire to tidy up the garden. Serve with lots of butter and perhaps crème fraîche with chives or tarragon. Create some Persian Toasted Nuts (see page 48) by placing the almonds on a piece of foil on the grill, sprinkle with salt and moisten them with lime juice. Or oil some slices of halloumi, wrap them in vine leaves and cook them over a hot grill for a few minutes on each side. You might like to throw some fresh herbs, such as thyme, over the coals close to the end of the kebabs' cooking time – their oils will add extra flavour.

A selection of charcoal-grilled vegetables, lightly basted in oil before being placed on the grill. Use fennel, artichokes, asparagus and charcoal-grilled baby leeks with Romesco Sauce *page 60*

Marinated Halloumi Kebabs *opposite page*

Grilled Courgette Salad *page 158*

Green salad of mixed young leaves with rocket

Poached peaches (leaving the skins on), sliced and wrapped in foil with lemon juice, honey and Cointreau and placed over the coals for about 10 minutes. Served with whipped cream *page 193*

TO DRINK

Organic dry cider, home-made lemonade sweetened with honey

marinated halloumi kebabs

As with roast vegetables, kebabs offer abundant variety, in that they can be made using seasonal ingredients. The choice I have used here conjures up a Mediterranean barbecue. Serve with Puy Lentil Salad with Lemon, Cumin and Herbs (see page 170) and Cucumber Raita (see page 145) or, alternatively, with a bowl of Aïoli (see page 256) and a slice of *Farinata* (see page 50) to mop up the juices.

SERVES 4

6 tablespoons olive oil
Grated zest and juice of 1 lemon
2 green chillies, deseeded and finely chopped
8 baby artichoke hearts or 1 × 400g can artichoke hearts, halved
200g halloumi, chopped into 2cm cubes
1 courgette, sliced thinly
16 small mushrooms, trimmed
16 cherry tomatoes
8 large garlic cloves
Salt and pepper
16 bay leaves (fresh if possible)

If you are using wooden skewers, soak them in water for half an hour before use. (You will need 8.)

Mix the olive oil, lemon juice and zest and green chillies in a bowl. Add the baby artichoke hearts, halloumi cubes, courgette slices, mushrooms, cherry tomatoes and garlic cloves, season and mix well with your hands. Leave for half an hour at room temperature to marinate.

Preheat the grill on a medium-high setting.

Thread the marinated vegetables and the bay leaves onto 8 medium-sized skewers, distributing each type of vegetable and halloumi equally across the skewers. The pieces should be barely touching one another, so do not pack them onto the skewers too tightly.

Place the skewers on a rack in a grill tray and grill, turning regularly and basting the vegetables with the marinade using a brush to stop them drying out. Cook until the vegetables are soft, 10–15 minutes. Serve at once.

VARIATIONS

— Substitute a red pepper, cut into 2.5cm chunks, for the courgette.
— Substitute tofu for the halloumi.

baked peppers with goats' cheese

This is a delicious and wonderfully easy recipe; the more sunny and sweet the peppers and tomatoes, the better the final result. Aim to find peppers which accommodate the diameter of the tomatoes elegantly. You can experiment with a wide variety of goats' cheeses: the softer ones will need less cooking.

SERVES 4

Olive oil, for greasing
2 large red or yellow peppers, halved vertically
2 large tomatoes, halved horizontally
2 garlic cloves, roughly chopped
200g goats' cheese, cut into 4 pieces
Basil leaves, to garnish

Preheat the oven to 180°C.

Grease a baking dish with olive oil and place the pepper halves on it, cut-sides down. Bake until the peppers have heated through and are starting to soften, about 12–15 minutes.

Remove from the oven and turn the peppers over. Nestle a tomato half in the hollow centre of each pepper. Bake until the tomatoes have softened, about a further 15 minutes.

Remove from the oven once again, spread the garlic on the tomatoes and place a piece of goats' cheese on top of each tomato. Bake until the cheese has melted, a further 5–10 minutes. Garnish with basil leaves and serve.

fennel gratin

Seventeenth-century writer and gardener John Evelyn writes of fennel: 'we have it from *Bolognia* but the sweetest and most aromatick comes from the *Azores*, hot and dry, expels Wind, sharpens the Sight, and recreates the Brain… The Italians eat the blanched Stalk all Winter long'. So do we.

SERVES 4

3 tablespoons olive oil
3 fennel bulbs, cut from stem to base into 2cm slices
400ml hot vegetable stock, made with
   1 teaspoon Marigold bouillon powder
½ teaspoon fennel seeds
100ml cream
Salt and pepper
50g Parmesan cheese, grated

Heat 2 tablespoons of the olive oil in a large frying pan over a medium heat and add a layer of sliced fennel. Cook, turning the fennel once, until it is golden, 2–3 minutes on each side. Repeat the process with the rest of the fennel slices and the remaining oil.

Preheat the grill on a high setting.

Put all the fennel back into the frying pan, cover with the stock and add the fennel seeds. Simmer until the fennel is tender, about 10 minutes. The liquid should be reduced to a syrupy sauce. Stir in the cream and let the sauce heat through. Season.

Place the mixture in an oven-proof dish and sprinkle the Parmesan over it. Grill until the cheese bubbles. Serve immediately.

VARIATION

Sauté 100g mushrooms, sliced, in 1 teaspoon olive oil. Add the mushrooms to the fennel when it is placed in the gratin dish before sprinkling on the Parmesan.

puy lentil gratin

Grown in the ancient volcanic Puy area of France, Puy lentils were the first vegetable to receive AOC (*Appellation d'Origine Contrôlée*). The lentil even has its own website (*www.lalentillevertedupuy.com*). It was known originally as *essaü*, because Esau was said to have given away his birthright for a dish of lentils in the *Book of Genesis*. When Cervantes introduces Don Quixote in his book of the same name, he explains that he ate 'lentils on Fridays' – the Catholic day of fasting.

This *Gratin de Lentilles Vertes du Puy* recipe came off a French Puy lentil packet bought in the Tarn about 25 years ago.

SERVES 4

280g Puy lentils
60g butter, plus extra
  for greasing
1 leek, chopped
2 onions, chopped

2 carrots, grated
150ml cream
170g Emmental cheese, grated
Salt and pepper
30g walnuts

Preheat the oven to 170°C. Grease a medium earthenware baking dish.

Overnight, or half a day before you want to use them, put the lentils in a large bowl and generously cover them with boiling water. The next day, drain and cook in fresh boiling water until tender, between 15 and 40 minutes depending on their age. Drain.

Meanwhile, melt the butter in a frying pan (which has a lid) over a low heat. Sweat the leek and onions in the butter for about 5 minutes, then add the carrot. Cook, covered, until soft, 10–15 minutes.

When cooked, mix together both the lentils and vegetables. Add 75ml of the cream and 120g of the Emmental. Season. Pour into the prepared baking dish.

Blend the nuts and the remaining cream and Emmental in a food processor and roughly spread the resulting nutty cream on top of the mixture in the baking dish. Bake until the gratin is hot and golden on top, about 30 minutes.

VARIATION

For a less rich version, substitute olive oil for the butter and coconut milk for the cream.

buckwheat crêpes with two fillings

A variety of filling goes hand-in-hand with the fun of making and eating pancakes, so below I give recipes for two fillings, each to fill six pancakes. Diners receive two crêpes, each with a different filling.

SERVES 6

12 Breton Buckwheat Pancakes (see page 278)
Butter, for greasing

SPINACH AND CREAM CHEESE FILLING

225g cooked spinach, chopped
225g goats' cream cheese
60g grated Parmesan cheese
2 eggs
Salt and pepper
Nutmeg

VEGETABLE AND EGG FILLING

2 slim leeks, chopped into short lengths
6 canned artichoke hearts, well drained and halved
6 tablespoons crème fraîche
12 cherry tomatoes, halved
6 small eggs or quails' eggs
90g Manchego cheese, grated
2 tablespoons chopped parsley

Heat the oven to 210°C. Line 2 large baking trays with buttered baking paper. Place 6 pancakes on each tray.

To make spinach and cream cheese filling, mix the spinach, cream cheese, 30g Parmesan and eggs in a bowl. Season with salt, pepper and a grating of nutmeg, to taste. Divide the filling equally between the 6 pancakes on 1 tray, leaving 3–4cm around the edges clear. Fold in the edges to form a square. Sprinkle with the remaining Parmesan.

To make the vegetable and egg filling, steam the leeks until tender. Lay the leeks and artichoke hearts on the remaining 6 pancakes, again, not too close to the edges, so they can be tucked over to keep in the filling. Spoon over some crème fraîche, lay the tomato halves on top, then break an egg over the vegetables on each pancake. Season with salt and pepper. Sprinkle with cheese. Fold over the edges to form a square.

Bake until the spinach mixture has puffed up and the Parmesan is golden, about 6 minutes, and the egg is thoroughly cooked, about 8 minutes. Sprinkle parsley over the vegetable and egg crêpes to serve.

weekday supper with friends

It is a great treat to relax with friends midweek after a day's work, so here is a supper designed to be put together easily. For eight people the amounts in the recipes will suffice, save that you will need to double quantities of the beans and baked peppers. Prepare the starters, the Catalan pears and the vanilla ice cream custard the night before and store in the fridge. On arriving home on the day of the supper, bring the starters and the Catalan pears to room temperature, and churn the ice cream custard in an ice cream maker and freeze. Prepare the beans save for the final five-minute heat up. Prepare the herby potatoes and cover with water. Now prepare the baked peppers up to the point of nestling in the tomatoes. Lay the table and place the starters in the centre with the crudités. Shortly before the guests arrive, make the Roquefort salad, set the potatoes to boil and the peppers and tomatoes to continue cooking. Just before you sit down to the starters, add the cheese to the peppers and tomatoes in the oven and begin to heat up the beans.

SERVES 8

For starters, Champignons à la Grèque, Broad Bean *Bissara* and Crudités for dipping *pages 53, 42 and 104–5*

For the main dish, Baked Peppers with Goats' Cheese, French Beans, Provençal Herby Potatoes and Roquefort and Walnut Salad *pages 84, 172, 184 and 149*

Catalan Pears Poached in Honey, Saffron and Vanilla with some Vanilla Ice Cream *pages 196 and 221*

TO DRINK

A light-bodied Beaujolais and a crisp Bordeaux Sauvignon Blanc, with plenty of sparkling water

spanish cauliflower cheese

Dating back to before the time of Christ, Manchego cheese is made from Manchega sheep's milk in the La Mancha plateau of central Spain, where Cervantes' Don Quixote of La Mancha tilted at windmills. Don Quixote was passionate about Manchego and declared 'Hunger is the best sauce in the world, and Manchego is the best gratification for hunger'. This cheese is excellent eaten as a tapas with Gordal olives.

Manchego has Protected Designation of Origin (PDO) status from the European Union, which states that it should be matured from between 60 days and 2 years. Traditionally it was made in plaited *esparto* grass baskets, which left a striking zig-zag pattern on the rind that is mimicked on today's moulds. Look for the image of Don Quixote on the rind.

Pepa, a Basque friend, cooked me this *Coliflor con Queso* when we shared a flat in Toledo, on the edge of the La Mancha region. It was the last year of Franco's life when Pepa's husband (a doctor, like Pepa) was billeted for military service. Every Sunday evening we were joined by a Catalan and Galician colleague and we would all share a splendidly drawn-out meal in lively discussion of the problems of the world – not least of Spain under Franco. (Pepa's abundant use of garlic influenced a dramatic change in my approach to cooking.)

SERVES 4

1 large cauliflower, broken into florets, discarding thick stalks
50g butter
35g potato flour
600ml milk
4 eggs
90g Manchego cheese, grated
Salt and pepper

Preheat the oven to 180°C.

Steam the cauliflower until it is al dente, about 8 minutes.

Using the butter, potato flour and milk, make a béchamel sauce following the instructions on page 258.

Meanwhile, whisk the eggs and add the cheese. Season.

Put the steamed cauliflower into a baking dish. Cover with the béchamel sauce, and then pour the egg-and-cheese mixture over the top. Bake until golden brown, about 20 minutes.

mushroom stroganoff

Stroganoff bears the name of one of the richest families in pre-revolutionary Russia, who were strong supporters of the arts. This recipe is found in Elena Molokhovets' classic book *A Gift for Young Housewives* (1861), which appeared at the time when celebrated French chefs, notably Antonin Carême, were enticed to St Petersburg and Moscow. Molokhovets continually revised her book; it went through more than 20 editions by 1917 and sold nearly 300,000 copies.

Russians are great mushroom hunters, so if you can lay your hands on wild mushrooms they would be especially appropriate for this recipe. Ceps are particularly valued. This stroganoff could be served either with *Kasha* (see page 188) or mashed potato.

SERVES 4

40g dried mushrooms
3 tablespoons olive oil
2 onions, thinly sliced
50g butter
500g chestnut mushrooms, trimmed and chopped
2 fat garlic cloves, finely chopped
150ml white wine
150ml soured cream
1 tablespoon sweet paprika
Squeeze of lemon juice
Salt and pepper
1 tablespoon chopped parsley

Immerse the dried mushrooms in boiling water and leave them to soak for 10 minutes. Drain (reserve the liquid for a soup).

Heat the oil in a pan and sweat the onions over a medium-low heat until soft, about 10 minutes. Add the butter and both the fresh and drained dried mushrooms to the onions. Fry until the liquid has evaporated and the mushrooms begin to take on colour.

Toss in the garlic and continue to cook gently. As the garlic turns golden, stir in the wine. Add the cream and paprika and simmer for 5–10 minutes until the sauce reduces and thickens. Add a squeeze of lemon and season to taste. Serve sprinkled with parsley.

sweet and sour tofu with oyster mushrooms

Tofu, made from soya beans, appears in a breathtaking variety of forms in China, including deep fried. Here it is served in cubes cut from larger blocks. This sweet and sour recipe is typical. Serve it on a bed of buttery mashed potato, which, while unconventional, complements the sweet and sour sauce beautifully.

SERVES 4

Grated zest of 1 lemon
4 tablespoons lemon juice
4 tablespoons tamari
2cm piece of ginger root, grated
5 garlic cloves, chopped
2 tablespoons honey
4 tablespoons tomato purée
6 tablespoons water
400g firm tofu, cut into 2.5cm cubes
1 tablespoon sunflower oil
250g broccoli, cut into florets
400g oyster mushrooms
200g cashew nuts, toasted

Put the lemon rind and juice, tamari, ginger, garlic, honey, tomato purée and water in a medium bowl and stir thoroughly. Add the tofu and leave to marinate at room temperature for 2 hours.

Heat the oil in a hot wok. Add the broccoli and mushrooms and stir-fry until lightly cooked, about 4–5 minutes. Reduce the heat to medium, pour in the tofu with its marinade and heat through thoroughly. Finally, add the toasted cashew nuts. Serve at once on mashed potatoes.

aubergine, sweet potato and green pepper curry

It was my Pakistani brother-in-law Suj who introduced me to this winning combination of aubergine, sweet potatoes and green pepper. It uses tamarind paste, which is easily found in Indian grocery shops.

SERVES 4

5 tablespoons sunflower or olive oil
½ teaspoon cumin seeds
½ teaspoon mustard seeds
¼ teaspoon fenugreek seeds
1 large onion, finely chopped
1cm cube of ginger root, grated
2 green chillies, deseeded and chopped
2 garlic cloves, chopped
2 teaspoons turmeric
2 teaspoons Garam Masala (see page 267)
400g tomatoes, chopped (or 1 × 400g can chopped tomatoes)
1 large aubergine, chopped into 2cm cubes
2 sweet potatoes, chopped into 2cm cubes
1 green pepper, sliced
250ml water
1 tablespoon tamarind paste
2 tablespoons lemon juice
1 tablespoon honey
Salt
Handful of fresh coriander, leaves picked and chopped

Heat the oil in a large pan over a medium heat and fry the seeds until they splutter and burst, about 1 minute. Mix in the onion, ginger, chillies and garlic. Fry over a medium-low heat until the onion is soft, about 10 minutes. Stir in the ground spices and cook briefly.

Add the tomatoes and fry until they begin to soften, about 5 minutes. Stir in the aubergine and simmer with a lid on for 15 minutes. Mix in the sweet potatoes and green pepper, add the water and simmer until the vegetables are soft, around 25 minutes. Season with tamarind paste, lemon juice, honey and salt. Sprinkle with fresh coriander to serve.

VARIATION

Substitute 2 waxy potatoes for the sweet potatoes.

GETTING
FANCY

softly boiled quails' eggs with mushroom purée on rösti

This dish has long been a family favourite for special occasions. It is inspired by a memorable meal in Adlard's restaurant: David Adlard created little tart bases for the others and omitted the pastry for me. My son Alex suggested that rösti would complete a grain-free alternative. All elements, save the sauce, can be prepared the day before and heated when ready to eat.

SERVES 4

8 quails' eggs
½ quantity Rösti (see page 187 and instructions below)
⅔ quantity Hollandaise Sauce (see page 257)
1 tablespoon finely chopped chives or parsley

MUSHROOM PURÉE

30g dried ceps
30g butter
60g shallots or onions, finely chopped
200g chestnut mushrooms, roughly chopped
250ml red wine
Salt and pepper
1 tablespoon cream

To make the mushroom purée, soak the ceps for 30 minutes. Drain.

Melt the butter in a pan and soften the shallots over a medium-low heat, about 5 minutes. Blend the mushrooms, ceps and shallots in a food processor, transfer to a pan, add the wine, season, and simmer gently to evaporate the liquid until the mixture is dry, about 30 minutes.

Meanwhile, boil the quails' eggs for exactly 2 minutes. Plunge into iced water and shell when cold. Refrigerate in cold water.

Shortly before the meal, prepare the Hollandaise sauce (see page 257) and keep it in a warm place. Then make 8 small rösti (see page 187) that are 5–6cm in diameter.

Meanwhile, stir the cream into the mushroom mixture and warm gently.

Once the rösti are ready, steam the quail's eggs for 20 seconds.

Take 4 small warm plates and place 2 rösti on each. Cover each rösti with some mushroom purée and nestle a quail's egg on top. Spoon some Hollandaise Sauce over each egg and sprinkle over some chives.

finger food for a cocktail party

Oh the tactile pleasure of touching the food – little edible sofas (*canapé* means 'sofa' in French) garnished with a delectable morsel perched on top. Martin Luther was once reputed to have cried out: 'God protect us from forks'. Your guests can easily pick from this spread as they enjoy conversation. *Skorthalia* is excellent on grilled aubergine for garlic lovers. Tortilla, cooled and chopped into diamonds (and garnished with a teaspoonful of Aioli and, in summer, a baby Slow-roasted Tomato or, in winter, an olive) is easy to pop into the mouth. Dips can be prepared in advance.

SERVES 20

Aubergine *Skorthalia* page 69

Tortilla garnished with Aïoli and Slow-roasted Tomatoes or olives pages 54, 256 and 260

DIPS

Try dipping roast asparagus or quails eggs into Aïoli, or Crudités into Red Pepper Purée or *Baba Ghanoush* pages 256, 104–5, 37 and 41

MISE EN BOUCHE OR FINGER FOODS

Small items to put in the mouth with fingers, such as good quality Kalamata or big juicy Spanish Gordal olives, Persian Toasted Nuts or Pakoras pages 48 and 137

TO DRINK

Campari, grapefruit juice and Prosecco cocktail. Make in a glass jug with 125ml Campari, 250ml grapefruit juice and 500ml Prosecco. Vary the proportions to taste!

canapés

For a spread of little parcels to pick up and pop into the mouth, there are many edible receptacles for the purées below. Little Gem lettuce leaves, small chicory leaves or a slice of cucumber are wonderfully light; roasted slices of aubergine or courgette or boiled new potato slices are substantial. One can hollow out a chunk of courgette, or create a slender boat of either baby aubergine or baby courgette, then grill or bake. Half a canned artichoke can be topped with a tiny dollop of Mayonnaise (see page 256).

For a party of 25, serve, along with a bowl of olives, 1 quantity of each of the recipes below, except the omelette, for which you will need a double quantity. Aim to make 1 courgette or aubergine roll per person.

CROWN PRINCE PUMPKIN AND RICOTTA CHEESE FILLING

Preheat the oven to 200°C. Deseed, slice and peel 500g pumpkin. Coat lightly in oil and lay on a baking tray, sprinkle with salt and roast until just soft, turning once, about 15 minutes. Do not to overcook or it will become watery. When cool enough to handle, press through a potato ricer or purée in a food processor. Leave to cool. Drain 50g Ricotta and mix with the cold pumpkin. Put a dollop of the mixture into the centre of a Little Gem or chicory leaf. In a frying pan, melt 3 tablespoons butter and fry 20 baby sage leaves. Place 1 leaf on top of the filling on each canapé.

TAPENADE

In a food processor, blend 200g stoned Kalamata olives, 50g capers, 1 tablespoon lemon juice, 90ml olive oil, the leaves from 2 sprigs of thyme and some pepper. Serve on a slice of cucumber or boiled new potato.

ASIAN ROLLED OMELETTE

Mix 3 beaten eggs, 2 finely chopped spring onions, 2 finely chopped red chillies, 2 tablespoons finely chopped coriander leaves, 2 teaspoons tamari and pepper. Heat 1 tablespoon oil in a 28cm frying pan and pour in the mixture. Tilt the pan to spread the mixture thinly to the edges. Cook until firm, 1–2 minutes. Slide the omelette onto a plate and roll it up into a long sausage. When cool, cut it on the diagonal into 1cm slices. (For a Korean variation place a sheet of toasted nori on the omelette before rolling up.)

AUBERGINE OR COURGETTE ROLLS

Slice strips of courgette or baby long thin aubergine with a mandoline. Brush with oil and chargrill on a griddle pan. Spread the lower two-thirds of each slice with goats' cream cheese mixed with chopped thyme or tarragon, lemon zest and black pepper, to taste. Roll up each slice, starting at the wider end. Secure with a cocktail stick.

blini

These blini are risen with bicarbonate of soda, with the aid of cream of tartar, rather than the original Russian yeast. They are easy to make and delicious.

Blini freeze well. Spread them on a tray and pop the tray in the freezer. Then, once they are frozen, take them off the tray, put them in a plastic bag and return them immediately to the freezer.

MAKES ABOUT 30 BLINI

2 eggs
350ml milk
200g buckwheat flour
30g butter, melted, plus extra for cooking
1 pinch of salt
½ teaspoon bicarbonate of soda
1 teaspoon cream of tartar

Beat the eggs with a hand-held blender. Add the milk, buckwheat flour and melted butter and beat to make a smooth batter. Add the salt, sieve in the bicarbonate of soda and cream of tartar and beat again to mix.

Heat a large, heavy frying pan and melt a little butter in it to give the base of the pan a thin covering. Pour in 1 tablespoon of the batter for each blini and spread it into a 5cm circle. Cook over a medium heat until the undersides are golden, about 1 minute. Turn over and cook until the second sides are golden, another 30 seconds. Add more melted butter for the next batch and repeat.

TOPPINGS

– A dollop of soured cream, garnished with Tapenade (see page 101) or with my sister-in-law Julia's excellent tomato concoction, made from 2 quantities Slow-roasted Tomatoes (see page 260), 600g fresh tomatoes, 90g purple onions and 12 sprigs of basil, all finely chopped and moistened with olive oil.
– A dollop of soured cream, garnished with Olive Pâté (see page 63) or with Pesto (see page 263).
– Mushroom purée garnished with a quail's egg (see page 98) and a teaspoon of Hollandaise sauce (see page 257).
– A beetroot and crème fraîche mixture. Use 1kg beetroot with their stalks and leaves. Separate the stalks and leaves from the beetroot, and either roast them (see page 179), or grate them and moisten with a little lemon juice, to taste. Wilt the leaves in a pan of boiling water.

Chop any large leaves and the stalks very finely across the grain. In 60g butter, fry 2 onions, chopped, then add the chopped stalks with 2 garlic cloves, chopped and cook over a medium-low heat until the stalks are soft, about 20 minutes. Finally, add the wilted leaves. Mix with 8 tablespoons crème fraîche. Spread on the blini, garnish with roasted sliced or raw grated beetroot.

— Crème fraîche mixed with caramelised shallots: slice 750g shallots and fry in 4 tablespoons olive oil over a low heat with a lid until lightly coloured, about 20 minutes. Add 3 tablespoons honey, increase the heat to medium and cook, uncovered, for 15–20 minutes until caramelised. Spread the mixture on the blini and put 1 tablespoon crème fraîche on top.

— Herby goats' cream cheese (see aubergine or courgette rolls, page 101).

— Hummus (see page 43), garnished with finely chopped chives, lemon zest and pomegranate seeds.

— Aubergine *Skorthalia* (see page 69), garnished with some finely chopped chives.

— Tzatziki: mix 670g thick Greek sheep's milk yogurt, 1 cucumber, peeled, deseeded and diced, 2 garlic cloves, finely chopped, and 2 tablespoons lemon juice, and garnish with dill or mint leaves.

sweet blini

Sweetened with just a little honey, blinis make an excellent little dessert. Simply follow the recipe above, adding 3 tablespoons honey to the beaten eggs with the milk, flour and melted butter before mixing into a smooth batter.

Top sweet blini with any of the suggestions below, or devise your own ideas. Fruits offer many possibilities.

TOPPINGS

— Maple syrup and a squeeze of lemon.
— Fruit purée.
— Whipped cream, garnished with fresh fruits such as wild strawberries, raspberries or blueberries and, perhaps, a dash of maple syrup.
— Goats' cream cheese with lemon and orange zest and juice and a drizzle of honey.
— For a birthday breakfast, try whipped cream with Cointreau and honey, garnished with raspberries and toasted flaked almonds.

crudités for dipping

A large plate of first-class vegetables for dipping, imaginatively presented, consisting of fresh, seasonal, organic produce, is a sight to behold. Have fun enticing your guests to sample its joys! Crisp pink radishes, baby courgettes, crunchy yellow-edged chicory, bright green asparagus, succulent young carrots and some generous sprigs of vine tomatoes, arranged in a burst of colour, are set to take centre stage.

The secret to success is to buy the very best quality. With a quantity of about 100g of vegetables in total per head and, basically, the more variety, the better. A farmers' market makes exciting hunting ground for this important quest and the vegetables are wonderfully fresh – the nearest you are likely to get to home-grown. Ideally, buy them in the morning of the day on which you wish to serve them or, at a pinch, the day before.

If the vegetables do need to be stored overnight, leafy vegetables such as lettuce and green vegetables like mangetout, asparagus and broccoli should be kept wrapped in damp kitchen paper in plastic bags at the bottom of the fridge. Vegetable leaves on their roots should not be separated until just before serving. Root vegetables and fennel should be stored in loosely fitting plastic bags, likewise in the bottom of the fridge. If you are fortunate enough to have a cool underground cellar, you can simply store your vegetables there with no extra hassle. Tomatoes, on the other hand, need to be stored at room temperature to preserve their flavour-producing enzymes. Herbs do well in the fridge door with their stems in a jam jar of water.

Below I provide ideas for preparation. Remember that the vegetables are finger foods, so present each in a suitable size and shape. Gone are the days of regimental lining up of dried-out carrot and celery sticks. Place all your vegetables in copious profusion on a beautiful plate. That being said, a little imperceptible taming to see that the colours are well spaced out and that the best parts of the vegetables are showing is fair play. You might like to nestle the bowls of dips in amongst the crudités.

PREPARATION SUGGESTIONS

– Baby artichokes: sliced, either left raw in lemon juice (see page 156) or lightly fried in olive oil.
– Asparagus: blanched and grilled (see page 60).
– Purple sprouting broccoli and cauliflower florets: raw if young enough, or blanched for 30 seconds in boiling water and then plunged into iced water.

— Carrots: peeled and cut into sticks if they are large. Present new carrots with 3cm stems left on.

— Chicory, Little Gem, radicchio: keep attached to their roots until as close as possible to serving. Then trim the bases and separate the leaves.

— Courgettes and cucumber: both are lovely served in sticks. I like the crunch and the colour of their green skin. Miniature courgettes from the garden look picturesque whole.

— Fennel: thinly sliced with a mandoline; cut any large bulbs in half before slicing.

— French beans: blanched for 30 seconds.

— Slim baby leeks: blanched and grilled (see page 60).

— Mangetout: remove strings and present them raw and untrimmed.

— Peppers: sliced into ribbons.

— Baby new potatoes: boiled.

— Radishes: served with leaves on if fresh.

— Cherry and small vine tomatoes: presented on the vine.

carrot and goats' cheese charlottes with cream sauce

Charlottes are made in a mould that is lined – here, in ramekins lined with strips of carrot. They appear to have been a late-eighteenth-century English creation, originally as a dessert, and were probably named in honour of George III's wife, Queen Charlotte. After Napoleon's defeat at Waterloo, the great French chef Antonin Carême (1784–1833) worked for the Prince Regent in London and Brighton. It seems that it was during this English sojourn that he made his acquaintance with the charlotte. His *charlotte à la parisienne* became a fashionable nineteenth-century dish throughout Europe.

I have made this delicious recipe for years. My son, Alex, chose it to cook for the BBC Radio Wales programme *Wales on the Menu*. This version benefits from the advice he was given by the Welsh food critic, Simon Wright, and the patron of London's Michelin-mentioned vegetarian restaurant Vanilla Black, Andrew Dargue. The vibrant colour of the carrots in the photo on the previous pages illustrates the quality of the vegetables we have been eating for the past 20 years out of our weekly box grown by vegetable farmers John and Yvonne, on their farm near Pencoed.

SERVES 6

500g carrots, roughly chopped,
    plus 1 carrot for lining
1 onion, roughly chopped
60g butter, plus extra for
    greasing
175ml vegetable stock, made
    with ¼ teaspoon Marigold
    bouillon powder
2 tablespoons chopped parsley
3 eggs and 1 extra yolk
150g soft goats' cheese
Nutmeg
Salt and pepper

CREAM SAUCE

280ml vegetable stock, made
    with ½ teaspoon Marigold
    bouillon powder
2 shallots, finely chopped
1 tomato, peeled and chopped
1 tablespoon balsamic vinegar
1 tablespoon honey
2 tablespoons chopped herbs,
    such as parsley, oregano and
    lemon thyme
Salt and pepper
140ml cream
60g butter

Preheat the oven to 180°C.

Using a potato peeler, cut strips from the extra carrot and place the strips in a bowl of boiling water for 2 minutes to soften. Butter 6 ramekins and line them with the carrot strips (see pages 106–7).

Blend the remaining raw carrots with the onion in a food processor.

Melt the butter in a pan and sweat the carrot mixture over a medium heat until it glistens, about 10 minutes. Add the stock and simmer on a low heat until the liquid has nearly disappeared, about 10 minutes. (This stage can be performed in the microwave on a high setting.)

Return the mixture to the food processor and blend with the parsley, eggs, egg yolk and cheese. Season with a grating of nutmeg and salt and pepper to taste. Divide between the lined ramekins.

Place the ramekins in a bain-marie (see page 15). Put it in the oven and cook until the charlottes are golden and there is slight shrinkage away from the sides of the ramekins, about 30 minutes.

Meanwhile, make the cream sauce. Mix all the ingredients except the cream and butter in a pan over a medium heat and cook until the mixture has reduced by half, about 10 minutes. Add the cream and butter and simmer until the butter has melted. Pour the mixture through a fine sieve so that you have a smooth sauce. Keep the sauce warm until you are ready to serve.

Turn out the charlottes onto hot plates and serve with the cream sauce.

VARIATION

Substitute 150g grated Manchego cheese for the soft goats' cheese.

aubergine 'cannelloni'

The first definitive reference to mozzarella cheese is in Bartolomeo Scappi's *Opera dell'Arte del Cucinare* (Venice 1570). Scappi cooked for six popes and revolutionised Italian cookery. His grand opus, which includes over 1000 recipes and extensive information about the equipment that a top cook would need in his kitchen, was reprinted until 1646. Scappi puts great emphasis on the freshness of ingredients and often uses chopped and sautéed onions, spring onions and garlic for flavour. He remarks that: 'dishes should be tasty and agreeable to the palate as well as pleasant and delightful to the eye with their pretty colours and appearance'; and he frequently comments on the importance of the cook's own opinion with phrases like 'depending on the judgement of the person making them', stressing that 'the cook must satisfy himself that he has done the best he can'.

Mozzarella continues to be popular to this day, and the combination of aubergine and mozzarella works extremely well, as can be seen by the number of classic dishes that pair up these ingredients, such as the well-loved *melanzane parmigiana*.

Aubergine cannelloni is excellent for dinner parties as it is delicious and rather fancy, with the added advantage of being a dish you can prepare in advance. Once you have poured the tomato sauce over the aubergine cannelloni, you can cover the dish with kitchen foil and set it aside. Then, twenty minutes before you intend to serve, put it into the oven as per the instructions below.

SERVES 4–6

2 aubergines (250g each)
150g mozzarella cheese
75g Parmesan cheese, grated
2 sprigs of rosemary, leaves picked
Butter, for greasing
4 tomatoes, each cut in half
1 large garlic clove, chopped
2 tablespoons olive oil, plus extra for greasing
Salt and pepper

Preheat the grill to high.

Cut the aubergines lengthways into 1cm slices. Brush both sides generously with olive oil and place on a lightly oiled baking sheet. Grill the aubergines until soft and golden, turning the aubergines once, about 8 minutes.

Meanwhile, combine the mozzarella, Parmesan and rosemary leaves in a food processor.

Preheat the oven to 170°C. Lightly butter a large earthenware baking dish.

Starting at the base of the aubergine slices (opposite to the end with the stalk), spread two-thirds of each aubergine slice with the cheese and rosemary mixture. Likewise, starting from the base, roll up each aubergine slice quite tightly, thereby enclosing the cheese mixture. Place the rolls in the prepared baking dish.

Place the tomatoes and garlic on a grill pan and sprinkle with the olive oil. Grill on a medium-high setting until soft, about 10 minutes. Blitz the grilled tomatoes and garlic in a food processor and season.

Pour the tomato sauce over the aubergine 'cannelloni' and bake, covered with foil, until cooked through, about 10 minutes, then cook uncovered to brown, a further 5 minutes.

VARIATION

Stuff the aubergine slices with 300g goats' Camembert, 75g grated Parmesan cheese, 60g chopped olives and the leaves from 2 sprigs of rosemary, finely chopped. Slice the Camembert and lay it on the roasted aubergine slices, sprinkle with some Parmesan, olives and rosemary. Roll up each aubergine slice and proceed as above.

imam bayildi

The name of the Turkish dish *imam bayildi* literally means 'the imam fainted'. One version of the story goes that when the imam's wife first served this dish, it was so delicious that he fainted with delight. Another version relates that the recipe used so much precious olive oil that the imam fainted at its cost and his wife's recklessness.

Tender, well-cooked aubergines are absolutely delicious, but you need to take care to ensure they are thoroughly cooked through at the initial frying stage. For parties at which I have offered a choice of main dishes, I have made this recipe using the small, long, thin Indian aubergines, which look lovely. They will heat through in the oven at 180°C in about 10 minutes.

SERVES 4

4 small to medium aubergines (200–250g each)
150ml olive oil, plus extra for greasing and sprinkling
4 onions, chopped into rings
4 garlic cloves, chopped into large pieces
250g tomatoes, chopped
150g tomato purée
60g pine nuts
60g raisins
Salt and pepper

Preheat the oven to 180°C. Grease a large baking tray with oil.

Leaving the stalks on and using a potato peeler, peel off strips of skin lengthways at intervals around the aubergines so that they end up looking striped. Heat three-quarters of the olive oil in a large frying pan over a medium heat and fry the whole, stripey aubergines, turning them until they are completely cooked, about 20 minutes.

Meanwhile, heat the remaining olive oil in another frying pan over a medium-low heat and soften the onions and garlic, about 10 minutes. Add the tomatoes and, when they are soft, about a further 10 minutes, add the tomato purée, pine nuts and raisins. Season.

Place the fried aubergines on the baking tray. Make a deep lengthways slit from the top to the bottom of each aubergine, avoiding cutting through the skin on the other side and leaving 1.5cm uncut at the top and bottom of the length. Open out the aubergine and stuff generously with the onion mixture. Sprinkle the aubergines with olive oil. Cover with kitchen foil. Bake until thoroughly cooked through, about 25 minutes, and then for another 5 minutes uncovered.

pumpkin gnocchi

Scrumptious pumpkin gnocchi drowned in butter and sage are eaten in Mantua, Northern Italy, during autumn when the pumpkins ripen. I imagine Claudio Monteverdi (1567–1643) devouring this dish before enchanting the influential Gonzaga family with his viol playing. Monteverdi considered his viol playing to be 'flowers' and his compositions as like 'fruit'.

For success with this recipe, you need to find a deep-orange, firm-fleshed pumpkin or squash, such as Crown Prince, the secret being to keep the pumpkin as dry as possible during cooking. Once the gnocchi are formed they can be left in the fridge for up to 24 hours before cooking, and they can be frozen. Gnocchi will keep for a fortnight in the freezer and then should be cooked from frozen.

SERVES 4–6

1kg squash
Salt and pepper
1 egg, beaten
90g Parmesan cheese, grated
Nutmeg
150g potato flour, plus extra for dusting
90g butter
4 sprigs of sage, leaved picked and chopped

Preheat the oven to 180°C.

Cut the pumpkin in half and deseed. Cut it into roughly 2.5cm-thick slices and peel. Lay them on a baking tray, sprinkle with salt and roast until just soft, about 20 minutes. Take care not to overcook the pumpkin or it will become watery. Leave to cool.

Once the roasted squash is cool enough to handle, press it through a potato ricer or purée it in a food processor. Transfer to a bowl and leave until cold.

Mix the beaten egg and 60g of the Parmesan into the cold pumpkin. Season with salt, pepper and a grating of nutmeg. Mix in the potato flour until you have a soft, light dough. Cover and leave in the fridge for 1 hour.

Dust a work surface with potato flour and place the gnocchi mixture on top, then flatten it into a square with a thickness of about 1.75cm. Cut this square into 1.5cm strips and roll each strip into a sausage. Cut the first sausage into 2cm lengths (see the photo on the opposite page).

Using a fork, press into each rectangle a little to flatten it and make attractive indentations on the top surface. Dust the gnocchi with potato flour and place them on a floured plate, ready to cook.

Half-fill a large saucepan of salted water and bring it to the boil. You will need to cook the gnocchi in several batches. Carefully spoon the gnocchi into the boiling water, trying to ensure they do not touch one another. Keep the water at simmering point. They are cooked when they rise to the surface, about 3–5 minutes. Using a slotted spoon, remove the gnocchi from the water and keep them warm on a serving dish in the oven set to 100°C while you cook subsequent batches.

Melt the butter and fry the sage leaves over a medium heat until crisp.

Serve the gnocchi immediately with the sage-leaf butter drizzled on top, sprinkled with the remaining Parmesan and some black pepper.

tuscan spinach and ricotta gnudi

Palline di Ricotta e Spinaci (spinach and ricotta balls) are a lighter cousin of gnocchi. They are also known in Florence as *gnudi* (naked) because they resemble a common filling for ravioli without the pasta. In this recipe of our ex-student and friend Giovanna, the *gnudi* are served smothered with butter and crispy sage leaves.

Success for light *gnudi* lies in thoroughly draining the spinach and ricotta; otherwise you will need to add extra potato flour to dry the mixture and aid in binding it, which makes them heavier – I use a tea towel to squeeze out the last drop of water from the spinach. It is also important to use fresh spinach for flavour and colour.

Giovanna introduced this recipe to us one evening and we all worked together to make it for supper, happily deciding that potato flour made a fine substitute for the traditional wheat flour. It was while staying with Giovanna in Tuscany that we tasted fresh ricotta, still warm from the ewes – one of the most perfect foods I have ever experienced. We ate it with local honey for a lazy breakfast in the sun amongst the cherry blossom.

SERVES 4

500g spinach
250g ricotta cheese, well drained over a sieve
15g Parmesan cheese, grated
1 egg
Salt and pepper

Potato flour, for coating
75g butter
6 sprigs of sage, leaves picked

Wash the spinach thoroughly, give it a shake and place it in a saucepan with some of the water still clinging to its leaves. Put on a lid and steam the spinach over a high heat until it wilts, about 2 minutes. Drain off any remaining water thoroughly and chop roughly.

Place the ricotta in a large bowl and mix with the spinach, Parmesan and egg. Season with salt, pepper and a grating of nutmeg. Cover and chill in the fridge for 1 hour.

Shape the spinach and ricotta mixture into little round dumplings that are about the size of walnuts in their shells. Roll them in potato flour to coat them.

Half-fill a large saucepan of salted water and bring it to the boil. You'll need to cook the *gnudi* in several batches. Carefully spoon the *gnudi* into the boiling water, trying to ensure they do not touch one another. Keep the water at simmering point. They are cooked when they rise to the surface, about 5 minutes. Remove them from the water with a slotted spoon. Keep the cooked *gnudi* warm in the oven set to 100°C. Repeat the same process until all the *gnudi* are cooked.

Meanwhile, over a medium heat, melt the butter and fry the sage leaves until crisp.

Serve the *gnudi* with the sage-leaf butter drizzled on top.

VARIATION

Substitute ½ quantity Tomato Sauce (see page 262) for the sage and butter and sprinkle with 2 tablespoons grated Parmesan cheese.

buckwheat pancakes filled with cheese fondue, with tomato coulis

This recipe from David Adlard transforms the simple crêpe into a sumptuous dinner party dish. All elements can be made in advance – the fondue will keep for up to a week in the fridge.

SERVES 4–6

1 quantity Breton Buckwheat Pancakes (see page 278)
Butter, for greasing
Basil leaves and snipped chives, to serve

CHEESE FONDUE

6 egg yolks and 2 egg whites
2 tablespoons Kirsch
250ml cream
½ teaspoon cumin seeds
½ teaspoon coriander seeds, crushed
250g Gruyère cheese, grated
250g Manchego cheese, grated
Pepper

TOMATO COULIS

1 tablespoon olive oil
2 garlic cloves, sliced
250g ripe tomatoes, skinned and chopped
Salt

To make the fondue, beat the egg yolks, Kirsch, cream and seeds together. Pour the mixture into a pan and cook over a low heat, stirring constantly, until it starts to thicken, 6–8 minutes. Do not let it boil. Take the pan off the heat and stir in the cheeses. Cool. Beat the egg whites until fluffy, then fold into the mixture. Grind in some pepper.

Line 2 large baking trays (28cm × 38cm) with buttered baking parchment. Heat the oven to 200°C.

Fold the pancakes in half, then in half again. Fill one of the pockets created in each pancake with the fondue. Place on the baking trays.

To make the coulis, heat the oil in a pan over a low heat and lightly fry the garlic, 2 minutes. Add the tomatoes. Cook over a medium heat until soft, 15 minutes. Blitz with a hand-held blender until smooth. Season.

Heat the pancakes in the oven until hot and slightly puffy, 15 minutes. Serve sprinkled with the herbs, with the hot tomato coulis.

festive family dinner

With three passionate cooks in the family, great joy is had
in discussing the finest details of Christmas dinner with all
the trimmings. Since my childhood there has been a tradition
of cooking whilst listening to the Christmas Eve carol
service of my father's college, Kings, on the radio.
Christmas Day afternoon is reserved for a bracing walk
up the Black Mountains to sharpen our appetites for the
ensuing feast. Then my sister and family arrive with the
soup and the occasion is further enriched by the company
of our international students. We welcome everyone
with an exquisite L'Olivera Cava – grown on a social-
integration cooperative whose members, people with
learning difficulties, participate in the entire wine-making
process – and some large green Gordal olives.

SERVES 8 TO 10

Clear Beetroot Soup *page 30*

Christmas Day Mock Goose *opposite page*

Mushroom Sauce *page 124*

Prune, olive and mushroom stuffing and
Cranberry Relish *pages 124 and 125*

Carrots, parsnips, potatoes and Roast
Jerusalem Artichokes *page 178*

Artisan cheeses with a salad of rocket,
young spinach and lettuce leaves

Christmas Bombe *page 230*

TO DRINK

Chilled L'Olivera Cava, a full-bodied Chateauneuf-
du-Pape to go with the mock goose, and a
fruity Gaillac doux for the bombe

christmas day mock goose

The habit of having something to carve for Christmas dinner appears to die hard, although I cannot help but feel that this is somewhat illogical for a vegetarian. Why should we hanker after a substitute for carving up the goose? Maybe we just need an excuse for the stuffing? The idea of a nut roast conjures up a dead weight for the digestive system, but this 'mock goose'– full of toasted cashews, sunflower seeds and French goats' cheese – puts the genre in a different light. The absurdity of the English eighteenth-century creation of mock turtle soup has always amused me, and Lewis Carroll's mock turtle in *Alice in Wonderland* is a splendid character. So why not a mock goose for Christmas?

Take care to ensure the mock goose is still moist when taken out of the oven. The accompaniments on the following pages go well with it and add to the festive spirit. We like to roast carrots, parsnips, Jerusalem artichokes and potatoes to complete the feast.

SERVES 8

Butter, for greasing
2 tablespoons olive oil
1 small onion, finely chopped
2 celery stalks, finely chopped
2 tablespoons chopped parsley
170g cashews, toasted and roughly chopped
85g walnuts, roughly chopped
85g ground almonds
85g cooked buckwheat
85g sunflower seeds
170g French goats' cream cheese
2 eggs
3 tablespoons tomato purée
1 tablespoon tamari
10g sweet paprika
Salt and pepper

Preheat the oven to 200°C. Line a 900g bread tin with buttered baking parchment.

Heat the olive oil in a frying pan over a medium-low heat and fry the onion and celery until soft, about 10 minutes. Place in a large mixing bowl and add all the other ingredients.

Pour the mixture into the prepared tin, cover loosely with baking parchment and cook until firm but still moist, about 50 minutes.

mushroom sauce

This creamy mushroom sauce with fresh tarragon beautifully complements the tasty Mock Goose.

SERVES 8

60g butter
1 onion, finely chopped
2 garlic cloves, chopped
400g white button mushrooms, finely chopped
2½ tablespoons potato flour
650ml hot milk
2 tablespoons tamari
2 tablespoons chopped tarragon
Black pepper

Melt the butter in a saucepan and soften the onions and garlic over a low heat, about 10 minutes. Stir in the mushrooms, increase the heat to medium and cook until soft, about 10 minutes. Take the pan off the heat.

Stir the potato flour into the mushroom mixture. Add the hot milk a little at a time, stirring constantly and vigorously until you have a smooth sauce. Add the tamari, tarragon and some black pepper. Serve immediately.

cranberry relish

This wonderfully simple and tangy relish offsets the Mock Goose brilliantly.

MAKES 8

200g frozen cranberries
1 orange, roughly chopped
90g honey

Combine all ingredients in a food processor. Check that there is enough honey to sweeten the relish. Leave overnight: the taste will develop as the cranberries thaw.

prune, olive and mushroom stuffing

This is our favourite stuffing and Christmas dinner would not be the same without it. Use the best green olives you can find.

SERVES 8

90g butter
200g mushrooms, sliced
225g prunes, stoned and chopped
160g green olives, pitted and chopped

Preheat the oven to 200°C.

In a frying pan, melt the butter and fry the mushrooms over a medium-low heat until soft, about 10 minutes. Mix in the prunes and olives and heat through, about 2 minutes.

Place the mixture in a small ovenproof bowl and cover with baking parchment. Heat through in the oven for 15 minutes before serving. (If you are serving this stuffing with the Christmas Day Mock Goose nut roast (see page 123), you can put it into the oven for the last 15 minutes of the cooking time for the nut roast.)

thai green curry with tofu and shiitake mushrooms

Uniquely in South East Asia, Thailand was never colonised, although there have been many outside influences. Its tropical monsoon climate produces an abundance of indigenous vegetables and fruit. The royal court has played an important role in promoting Thai cuisine; Thai kings themselves have written cookery books, including a genre specifically dedicated to funeral feasts. Thai food is full of contrasts: crunchy, soft, sweet, sour, hot or cool. Great attention is paid to presentation, enhanced by graceful vegetable carvings.

Thai cuisine uses many spices and vegetables that are generally unavailable in the West. But, nowadays, frozen Kaffir lime leaves can often be found in Chinese supermarkets and they make a great difference to the authentic freshness of this curry. If you are in luck you will find coriander sold complete with its roots; otherwise I suggest you use 12 coriander stems. The recipe produces more green curry paste than you need for the curry, but bear in mind that the paste freezes well or it will keep in a jar in the fridge for a fortnight. Consider making it in bulk and freezing it, ready for use in this dish.

SERVES 8

2 × 400ml cans coconut milk
600g aubergines, halved and sliced into half moons
300g shiitake mushrooms, thickly sliced
300g chestnut mushrooms, thickly sliced
300ml hot vegetable stock, made with
   ½ teaspoon Marigold bouillon powder
1 lemongrass stalk, bruised
6 Kaffir lime leaves
1 tablespoon and 1 teaspoon tamari
400g broccoli florets
600g firm tofu, cut into 2.5cm cubes
Juice of 1 lime (use the zest for the paste)
2 tablespoons plus 1 teaspoon honey
Small handful of coriander, leaves picked and chopped

GREEN CURRY PASTE (MAKES ABOUT 225G)
5–10 green chillies, roughly chopped
4 garlic cloves, roughly chopped
2 lemongrass stalks, outer leaves removed and stems sliced thinly
2 shallots, chopped

2.5cm cube galangal or ginger root, thinly sliced
6 fresh coriander roots or 12 coriander stems, roughly chopped
2 Kaffir lime leaves
Grated zest of 1 lime
2 teaspoons coriander seeds, crushed
1 teaspoon cumin seeds, crushed
1 teaspoon black peppercorns, crushed
½ teaspoon salt
4–5 tablespoons water

Combine all the ingredients for the green curry paste in a food processor, adding water a tablespoon at a time to create a thick paste, about 4–5 tablespoons in total.

To make the curry, gently open the cans of coconut milk and spoon off 10 tablespoons of the thicker cream that will have risen to the top of the cans. Put this cream in a large lidded casserole dish. Reserve the milk. Set the casserole dish of coconut cream on the stove over a moderately hot heat and, when it has transformed into hot oil, add 150g of the green curry paste and fry to temper it, (see page 15); it is ready when the oil separates and the paste turns golden, about about 2–3 minutes.

Reduce the heat to medium, add the aubergines and mushrooms and toss them in the paste until it has been well absorbed, about 3 minutes. Add the reserved coconut milk, the stock, lemongrass, Kaffir lime leaves and tamari and bring to the boil. Then reduce to simmering point and cook the aubergines and mushrooms, about 8 minutes. Put in the broccoli and, when it is al dente, add the tofu to heat through. Add the lime juice and enough honey to counterbalance the sourness of the lime. Serve sprinkled with coriander leaves.

summer vegetable tagine

Meltingly tender and aromatic, this Moroccan stew takes its name from the heavy earthenware dish in which it is made, which consists of a flat circular base with low sides and a high pointed cover to encourage condensation to fall back into the stew. When the stew is cooked the sizzling tagine base goes straight to the table for serving. Often, pottery tagine dishes are glazed and decorated with elegant patterns. Originally a Berber dish, Eastern spices, such as cinnamon, ginger, cumin and saffron were adopted with the arrival of the Arabs in the seventh century.

This recipe makes the most of summer vegetables, and below I provide a variation for winter. But it is a recipe with almost unlimited potential for creative variation, so let seasonal produce be your guide.

SERVES 8

6 tablespoons olive oil
3 onions, finely chopped
2 cinnamon sticks (each 10cm in length)
1cm cube ginger root, finely grated
4 garlic cloves, chopped
2 teaspoons ground cumin
2 teaspoons ground coriander
2 teaspoons sweet paprika
2 green chillies, chopped, or 2 tablespoons harissa
Rind of 1 preserved lemon, rinsed and finely diced
1 good pinch of saffron
4 ripe tomatoes, finely chopped, or 400g can chopped tomatoes
500g carrots, cut into 6cm lengths
600g small waxy potatoes (halved if over 5cm in length)
2 large fennel bulbs, trimmed and cut vertically into 2cm slices
1 aubergine, chopped into 2.5cm cubes
1 courgette, chopped into 2cm thick rounds
1 red pepper, chopped
1 litre stock, made with 2 teaspoons Marigold bouillon powder
20 small black olives
Juice of 1 lemon
Generous handful of coriander
Generous handful of parsley, plus a sprig to garnish
Salt

In a large casserole (cast iron works well) or a tagine, if you have one, heat the oil over a low heat and sweat the onions, stirring regularly, until soft, about 15 minutes. Then stir in the cinnamon sticks, ginger, garlic,

cumin, coriander, paprika, chillies, preserved lemon rind and saffron. Add the tomatoes, carrots, potatoes, fennel, aubergine, courgette and pepper and cover with stock. Bring to the boil, then simmer until meltingly soft, about 2½ hours.

Add the olives, lemon juice, coriander and parsley. Season. Simmer for 1 minute and serve, garnished with the parsley sprig.

VARIATIONS:

— In winter, substitute 300g pumpkin, half a head of celery (chopped into 6cm lengths) and 3 leeks (chopped into 6cm lengths) for the aubergine, courgette and pepper.
— Add 75g dried apricots half an hour before the end of the cooking time.
— Add 300g cooked chickpeas about 15 minutes before the end of the cooking time.
— For a quick version, chop all the ingredients very small and cook for 1 hour.

mushroom daube

This rich Provençal stew is traditionally made in a deep pot with a lid, a *daubière*, and it is often served with mashed potato. The name *daube* comes from the Italian *addobbo*, meaning seasoning, and refers to this method of cooking with aromatics and wine to enrich the flavour. Before the nineteenth century the term did not necessarily imply the inclusion of meat, as it generally has done subsequently.

Ideally a *daube* is cooked early in the morning or even the previous day to enable the flavours to develop fully in the red wine. I enjoy using a wide variety of mushrooms, such as chestnut mushrooms, oyster mushrooms, ceps, chanterelles and also some Asian shiitake. Serve this dish with mashed potato, pressed through a potato ricer and finished with lots of butter, a little milk, salt and a generous amount of black pepper.

SERVES 8–10

30g dried mushrooms (use ceps if available)
5 tablespoons olive oil
400g shallots or red onions, chopped
4 garlic cloves, chopped
800g very ripe tomatoes, chopped or 2 × 400g cans chopped tomatoes
1 celery stick, finely chopped
3 carrots, sliced into 3cm chunks

500ml red wine
12 black peppercorns
2 tablespoons grated orange zest
3 bay leaves
6 sprigs of thyme, leaves picked
8cm cinnamon stick
100g best-quality black olives (such as Kalamata)
900g fresh mushrooms
30g butter
2 tablespoons chopped parsley
½ lemon
Salt and pepper

Cover the dried mushrooms in boiling water and leave to soak for at least 10 minutes.

Heat the 4 tablespoons of the oil in a large, heavy casserole (which has a lid) over a medium heat and fry the shallots and garlic until soft, about 10 minutes. Add the tomatoes, celery and carrots and cook for a further 10 minutes. Now add the soaked mushrooms, then pass their soaking liquid through a sieve (it can be gritty) into the mixture. Add the wine, peppercorns, orange zest, bay leaves, thyme leaves and cinnamon stick. Cover the casserole pan with a circle of baking parchment and seal with a tightly fitting lid. Simmer until the carrots are meltingly soft, about 1½ hours. Take the casserole off the heat, add the olives and leave to stand for at least 4 hours to allow the flavours to develop.

Half an hour before the meal, reheat the *daube* sauce and simmer over a low heat. Chop any exceptionally large mushrooms in half, otherwise leave them whole. Fry the mushrooms in 3 batches in a large frying pan so that they are not crowded in the pan. For each batch, heat 1 teaspoon of the remaining oil in the frying pan over a low heat and gently fry the one-third of the mushrooms until they colour, about 8–10 minutes. Then add 10g butter, stir the mushrooms around so that they absorb it, about 1–2 minutes. Just before each batch is ready, add one-third of the chopped parsley and a squeeze of lemon juice.

Before serving the *daube*, add the cooked mushrooms to the casserole, season and heat through.

spinach roulade

Spinach roulade is a favourite family festive dish, served up for birthdays or, in an expanded version, cooked on an oven tray, for a memorable after-concert party under the stars to round off one of the music courses we have held at our home in Marnaves. This dish can be prepared up to a day in advance and then heated up half an hour before serving. It is equally delicious served cold for a special picnic. I like to use the creamy French goats' cream cheese that comes in little plastic tubs.

SERVES 6

Butter, for greasing
60ml cream
1 quantity Tomato Sauce (see page 262)

ROULADE BASE

1 quantity Béchamel Sauce (see page 258), made using
   only 400ml milk for a thicker sauce
¼ teaspoon freshly grated nutmeg
5 eggs, separated
60g Parmesan cheese, grated
60g Manchego cheese, grated

FILLING

500g spinach
60g butter
125g shallots or red onions, chopped
Salt and pepper
250ml goats' cream cheese

Preheat the oven to 200°C. Line a large Swiss roll tin (it should be 28cm × 38cm) with baking parchment (a little butter helps to stick it down) and lightly butter the baking paper itself.

To prepare the roulade base, make a béchamel sauce following the instructions on page 258, adding the nutmeg to the sauce with the seasoning. Mix in the egg yolks and half the grated cheeses.

Beat the egg whites until stiff, then gently fold into the cheese sauce with a metal spoon. Pour the mixture into the prepared tin and sprinkle the remaining cheese on the top. Bake until brown and puffy, about 15 minutes. Remove the roulade base from the oven and leave it to cool. Reduce the oven temperature to 160°C, ready to heat through the rolled-up roulade.

While the roulade base is cooking, wash the spinach thoroughly. Dry it in a salad spinner and chop it up, removing any tough stalks.

Melt the butter in a saucepan over a medium heat and soften the shallots, about 10 minutes. Add the spinach, season and cook until the spinach is soft and buttery – the time it takes will depend very much on the type of spinach being used: baby spinach leaves will wilt in 2–3 minutes, whereas older spinach leaves (equally tasty) could take up to 8 minutes.

Cover the cooled roulade base with a tea towel. Holding the tin at the sides, with the tea towel held taut across the top of the tin, deftly flip it over so that the roulade base ends up face-down on top of the tea towel on your work surface. Remove the tin and gently peel off the baking parchment.

If necessary, reposition the tea towel so that one of the longer edges of the roulade base is closest to you and parallel to the edge of the surface at which you are working. Spread the goats' cream cheese over the base, leaving a 2cm gap along the longer edge of the roulade base that is furthest from you. Cover the cheese with the spinach mixture. To roll up, begin by rolling over the long edge of the base that is closest to you, then continue rolling away from you, lifting up the tea towel to push the roll along and keep it tight (see the final picture on the opposite page). Any filling that is pushed along the base as you roll will end up on the gap you left uncovered at the far end of the base, but if any of the filling spills over the edge, gently tuck it back in. Carefully transfer the roulade to a large ovenproof dish or baking tray, using the tea towel to lift it.

Using a spatula, carefully spread the cream over the roulade, cover loosely with kitchen foil and heat through thoroughly, about 25 minutes. Serve with the tomato sauce.

VARIATIONS

– Add a good pinch of cayenne pepper to the béchamel sauce in place of the nutmeg.
– Substitute 350g cooked sliced mushrooms for the spinach and add to the melted shallots. Use a variety of types of mushrooms and perhaps add a few dried mushrooms, soaked in water for half an hour, to intensify the flavour.
– Add 25g fresh green peppercorns (available in brine) and 30g chopped pitted black olives to the béchamel sauce. In place of the goats' cream cheese and spinach filling, substitute 350g Taleggio cheese. Slice it and lay it, rind and all, over the roulade; dot with 200g Slow-roasted Tomatoes (see page 260), then roll up.

an indian feast

My kids were always allowed to choose the menu for supper
on their birthdays and, inevitably, they chose an Indian feast.
Small white or chestnut mushrooms make wonderfully
succulent pakoras to whet appetites (if they are medium sized,
chop them in half). The lemony spiced cashew nut stuffing
for the baby aubergines is delicious, authentic home Indian
cookery; place the Cucumber Raita nearby on the table as the
two go well together. Indian paneer cheese is easily available
both in Indian shops and supermarkets; it is excellent shallow-
fried, sprinkled with spices and mixed with spinach and
cream. For me, Dal is an essential part of any Indian meal.
Saffron, cardamom and rosewater flavour the yogurt
exotically in *Shrikhand* and if in season (April to June)
serve some sweet Alphonso mangoes alongside.

SERVES 8

Mushroom Pakoras *opposite page*

Indian Stuffed Baby Aubergines *page 140*

Saag Paneer *page 139*

Bhindi *page 143*

Dal *page 142*

Cucumber Raita *page 145*

Raw Green Mango Chutney *page 269*

Ripe Alphonso mangoes, if in season, and
Indian Yogurt Dessert *page 215*

TO DRINK

Indian Cobra beer, a fruity Australian
Hunter Valley Chardonnay, home-made
limeade sweetened with honey

pakoras

Pakoras, also known as bhajis, are a favourite Indian and Pakistani snack. They are at their best immediately from the fryer, but are also good served cold for a picnic. We enjoy them on long car journeys. You can envelop a wide variety of vegetables and even some fruits in the batter. Serve Pakoras with Raw Green Mango Chutney (see page 269) or Cucumber Raita (see page 145).

SERVES 8

Sunflower oil, for deep-frying
About 250g vegetables: onions (finely sliced into rings), small button mushrooms (whole, trimmed), small aubergines (cut horizontally into 1cm-thick rounds; cut the rounds into half moons if the diameter of the round is larger than 5cm), potatoes (finely sliced and parboiled), cauliflower florets (parboiled), plantain (in chunks), ripe banana (in chunks) and apple (peeled and sliced)

PAKORA BATTER

250g chickpea flour
½ teaspoon bicarbonate of soda, sieved
1 tablespoon ground coriander
2 teaspoons ground cumin
1 garlic clove, finely chopped
1 green chilli, finely chopped
½ teaspoon turmeric
1 pinch of asafoetida
½ teaspoon salt
2 tablespoons sunflower or olive oil
About 250ml water

To make the batter, put all the dry ingredients and the oil into a large bowl. Using a hand-held blender, mix in the water slowly until you have a smooth batter with the consistency of yogurt.

Heat the oil in a deep-fat fryer on a medium-high heat. Dip a handful of prepared vegetables in the batter. Lift them out one by one, allowing excess batter to drip back into the bowl, and place in a frying basket in a single layer without letting them touch one another. Lower the basket into the hot oil and fry until golden brown, about 2–3 minutes. Drain on kitchen paper. Taste a pakora to check you have the correct heat to cook the vegetables right through to the middle. Keep warm in an oven set to 100°C as you fry subsequent batches. If you wish to eat your pakora hot later, reheat them in an oven at 150°C for about 10 minutes.

aloo gobi

Serve this comforting dish with Indian Chickpea Flour Pancakes (see page 49) and some Cucumber Raita (see page 145) or, for a quicker meal, simply with some Dal (see page 142).

SERVES 4

300g waxy potatoes, cut into 2.5cm pieces
1 teaspoon ground coriander
½ teaspoon ground cumin
1 teaspoon turmeric
120ml water
6 tablespoons sunflower or olive oil
½ teaspoon cumin seeds
½ teaspoon mustard seeds
2cm piece of ginger root, grated
4 garlic cloves, finely chopped
2 red chillies, deseeded and chopped
600g cauliflower florets, cut in half lengthways
250g tomatoes, chopped
Approximately 2 tablespoons lemon juice
Salt
Small handful of coriander, leaves picked and chopped

Parboil the potatoes for about 5 minutes. Drain.

Meanwhile, mix the ground coriander, ground cumin and turmeric with the water in a bowl.

Heat the oil in a large saucepan over a medium heat and temper the cumin and mustard seeds (see page 15). When they begin to splutter, add the ginger, garlic and chillies and mix thoroughly. Then add the cauliflower florets and fry over a medium-high heat, stirring regularly, until they start to brown, about 5 minutes.

Reduce the heat to medium-low and stir in the spiced water and the potatoes. Cover the pan and simmer for about 8 minutes.

Stir in the tomatoes and simmer until the tomatoes are soft and the cauliflower is just cooked, about 8 minutes, adding a little more water if necessary to prevent the curry drying out. Add lemon juice and salt to taste.

Sprinkle the chopped coriander over the curry and serve.

saag paneer

This creamy saag paneer is a family favourite. I find that spinach asks for a little cream or crème fraîche, and that infusing paneer cheese with the complex flavour of garam masala (although cayenne pepper is another possibility) makes for a delicious dish.

SERVES 6

3cm cube of ginger root, peeled and roughly chopped
5 garlic cloves, chopped
1 green chilli, deseeded and chopped
4 tablespoons water
6 tablespoons sunflower or olive oil
225g paneer cheese, cut into 2cm cubes
1 tablespoon Garam Masala (see page 267)
Salt
750g spinach
100g cream
2 tablespoons chopped coriander

Blend the ginger, garlic and chilli with the water in a mini chopper until you have a smooth purée.

Heat 3 tablespoons of the oil in a saucepan over a medium heat and fry the paneer cubes until they are golden, turning them over as they cook, about 4 minutes. Remove from the pan and drain on doubled-up kitchen paper. Sprinkle with garam masala and a little salt.

Thoroughly wash the spinach, dry it in a salad spinner and chop it.

Heat the remaining oil in a saucepan over a medium heat and fry the spicy purée, stirring it well, until it colours, about 30 seconds. Add the spinach and stir it in well. Reduce the heat to medium-low, cover the pan and gently cook the spinach until it is soft, about 2–3 minutes. Add the cream, heat through and lightly season with salt (but take into account the fact that the paneer you will soon add to this mixture already has salt on it). Finally, mix in the paneer and serve garnished with coriander.

VARIATION

Substitute tofu for the paneer.

indian stuffed baby aubergines

If you are lucky enough to have an Indian or Middle Eastern shop nearby, you might find it sells several varieties of aubergine, including a baby long, thin type. This is the type to buy for this recipe.

SERVES 6–8

4 tablespoons sunflower oil
3 tablespoons chickpea flour
240g cashew nuts, ground
1 chilli, finely chopped
1 teaspoon grated ginger root
2 teaspoons ground cumin
1 teaspoon ground coriander
Large handful of coriander, leaves picked and finely chopped
4 tablespoons lemon juice
Honey
Salt
18 baby long, thin aubergines
1 teaspoon mustard seeds
1 teaspoon cumin seeds
1 teaspoon fenugreek seeds
600g tomatoes, chopped

Heat 1 tablespoon of the oil in a saucepan over a low heat and fry the chickpea flour gently until it starts to colour, about 2–3 minutes, being careful not to burn it. Take the pan off the heat and add the cashew nuts, chilli, ginger, ground cumin, ground coriander and fresh coriander and mix together. Season with the lemon juice, and also with honey (I usually add about 2 tablespoons) and salt, to taste.

Cut a deep cross in each aubergine – first make a lengthways slit, keeping 1cm uncut at both the stem end and base of the fruit, and cutting most of the way into the aubergine but ensuring you do not cut straight through into the skin on the other side. Next, make a short sideways slit at about half-way down the length of the fruit, across the first slit you made. One by one, open out the aubergines, taking care not to tear any uncut flesh, and stuff with the nut mixture; this takes a little persuasion.

Heat the remaining oil in a frying pan over a medium heat and temper the mustard, cumin and fenugreek seeds (see page 15). Add the tomatoes and heat through. Place the stuffed aubergines into the sauce, taking care not to dislodge the filling, and cook, covered, until tender, about 20 minutes.

dal

Nutritious and cheap, dal is the backbone of an Indian meal. It goes wonderfully with any vegetable curry and a salad of tomato, cucumber and green pepper chopped into 1.5cm chunks, with a good handful of chopped coriander and lime or lemon juice.

SERVES 6

6 tablespoons sunflower oil
4 teaspoons mustard seeds
2 teaspoons cumin seeds
2cm cube of ginger root, grated
2 green chillies, finely chopped
4 garlic cloves, finely chopped
2 teaspoons turmeric
400g red lentils
750ml boiling water
4 tablespoons lemon juice
4 thin slices of lemon
Salt and pepper
Generous handful of coriander, leaves picked
    and finely chopped

Heat the oil in a saucepan over a medium heat and temper the mustard and cumin seeds (see page 15). Add the ginger, chilli, garlic and turmeric and cook for 1–2 minutes. Stir the red lentils into the spices and give them a minute to absorb the flavours, then add the boiling water and bring to the boil. Simmer until the lentils are soft, about 25 minutes.

Take the pan off the heat, stir in the lemon juice and lemon slices, then season. Finally, stir in the coriander leaves and serve.

VARIATION

Make a vegetarian Mulligatawny soup to serve 4 by halving the all the ingredients but adding 2 litres water instead of 750ml. Mulligatawny is one of the most famous culinary results of British rule in India. It came into being through the relationship between the British officers' wives and their Indian cooks. British officers expected a preliminary soup course, which is not an Indian concept as Indians generally serve the entire meal together. Mulligatawny is a corruption of the Tamil *milagu tannir*, meaning pepper water, and in the Madras Presidency the British officials were known as 'mulls' after the soup.

bhindi

Many Indian dishes are full of complex spices and, to counterbalance this, I like to cook my *bhindi* simply. *Bhindi* are known in Britain as okra or ladies' fingers. Choose young and succulent *bhindi*. To prepare *bhindi*, wash them carefully under running water and pat them dry thoroughly with kitchen paper before you cut them. Chop off the conical caps but leave the elegantly pointed ends intact.

Watch that you do not overcook the *bhindi* as they will disintegrate and the dish will be spoilt. Stop cooking if there is any hint of sliminess at all.

I like to serve *bhindi* either alongside Sag Paneer (see page 139) and Dal (see opposite page) or they go excellently with Indian Chickpea Flour Pancakes (see page 49) and Cucumber Raita (see page 145).

SERVES 4

1 tablespoon sunflower or
   olive oil
1½ teaspoons mustard seeds
175g tomatoes, chopped small
500g *bhindi* (okra), cleaned and trimmed (see above)
30g butter
Salt and pepper

Heat the oil in a large frying pan (which has a lid) over a medium heat and temper the mustard seeds (see page 15). Add the tomatoes and cook until they become soft, about 5 minutes.

Add the *bhindi* and butter, cover the frying pan with a lid and cook gently over a medium-low heat until tender, about 15 minutes. Season and serve.

pumpkin and spinach masala

Masala means 'spice mixture'. In this recipe the pumpkin is partially cooked quite rapidly, then finished by simmering slowly in the spices until it has absorbed their flavour and become soft.

Serve with *Bhindi* (see page 143), Indian Chickpea Flour Pancakes (see page 49) and the chutney of your choice (see pages 268–9).

SERVES 4–6

750g pumpkin, peeled and
  chopped into bite-sized cubes
1 teaspoon turmeric
310ml coconut milk
250g spinach
2 green chillies, deseeded and
  roughly chopped
2cm cube of ginger root, grated
2 small onions,
  roughly chopped
2 large garlic cloves,
  roughly chopped
1 teaspoon coriander seeds
¼ teaspoon fennel seeds

¼ teaspoon green
  cardamom seeds
1 clove
2 tablespoons butter
½ teaspoon cumin seeds
1 teaspoon mustard seeds
1 sprig of curry leaves
1 5cm cinnamon stick
4 small tomatoes, finely
  chopped
Juice of ½ lemon
Salt and pepper
2 tablespoons chopped
  coriander leaves

Put the pumpkin in a large saucepan with the turmeric and 220ml of the coconut milk. Parboil on a medium to high heat, about 8 minutes.

Meanwhile, wash the spinach, dry it in a salad spinner and chop it.

In a mini chopper, grind the chillies, ginger, onions and garlic with the remaining coconut milk.

Put the coriander seeds, fennel seeds, green cardamom seeds and the clove in a mortar and crush them with a pestle. (Alternatively, grind them in a coffee grinder.)

Melt the butter in a saucepan over a medium heat, add the cumin seeds and mustard seeds, crush the curry leaves into the pan with your hands (which releases their flavour), and temper the spices (see page 15). When the seeds begin to splutter, add the paste you made with the chilli, ginger, onion and garlic and fry, stirring, over a medium to low heat, for about 1½ minutes. Add the crushed seeds and clove powder from the mortar along with the stick of cinnamon and fry until the paste is golden. Finally, add the tomatoes and cook, stirring from time to time, until they are soft, about 5 minutes.

Add this spicy mixture to the pumpkin, then stir in the spinach. Cover and simmer over a low heat until the pumpkin is cooked and the spinach has wilted, about 10 minutes. If the sauce becomes too thick, add more coconut milk. Leave the curry to cool, then refrigerate for several hours, or even overnight, to allow the flavours to develop.

Before serving, reheat the curry over a gentle heat, then take the pan off the heat and season with lemon juice, salt and pepper. Stir in the chopped coriander leaves and serve.

cucumber raita

Yogurt is a Turkish word, used in the West because yogurt reached Western Europe via Turkey and the Balkans. The enjoyment of a side dish of yogurt, cucumber and mint stretches from India to Greece. I love the combination of rosewater and crushed coriander seeds in this recipe.

Raita is excellent spread on slices of fried aubergine, perhaps decorated with pomegranate seeds, and makes a wonderful accompaniment to many Indian dishes.

SERVES 4–6

200ml thick goats' or sheep's yogurt
1 cucumber, finely sliced
½ small green chilli, deseeded and chopped
2 tablespoons rosewater
1 teaspoon coriander seeds, crushed
4 sprigs of mint, leaves picked and chopped
Salt and pepper

Put the yogurt in a bowl and mix in all the other ingredients. Season to taste.

VARIATION

Other additions could be finely chopped garlic, some grated ginger root, 1 teaspoon cumin seeds.

SALADS
AND SIDES

grilled goats' cheese salad with honey

Salade de chèvre chaud aux pommes has recently become popular in South-West France with apples replacing the conventionally used toast. When I am back in Wales I love the nutty flavour of Egremont Russet apples, which have been popular since Victorian times, for this recipe. My second choice would be Cox's Orange Pippins. If you can find it, the hard *Crottin de Chavignol* cheese, from the Loire, grills well.

SERVES 4

2 small Egremont Russet apples
150g goats' cheese log or *Crottin* cheese, with rind
80g mixed leaf salad
40g rocket
3 tablespoons olive oil
1 tablespoon lemon juice
2 tablespoons aromatic honey

Preheat the grill on a high setting.

Thinly slice the apples vertically to a thickness of about 5mm, avoiding the core, allowing 3 slices per person. If the diameter of the apple slices is much larger than that of the cheese, cut them in half, into half moons. Slice the goats' cheese into disks about 1.5–2cm thick. Place the apple slices on a baking dish and put a cheese disk on top of each one. Grill until golden, 1–2 minutes.

Mix the leaf salad and rocket in a bowl. Make a vinaigrette with the olive oil and lemon juice and dress the salad leaves. Lay on a serving plate. Place the apple slices with grilled cheese on top on the salad.

Gently heat the honey in a pan over a low heat, or in a microwave on a medium setting, for a very short time until hot and liquid. Pour the liquid honey over each slice of cheese. Serve immediately.

roquefort and walnut salad

Salade au roquefort et noix is a favourite in the Tarn region of France, where the noble walnut tree is plentiful. Archaeologists have found the remains of walnuts in the south of France dating back to 15000 BC.

Walnuts make a beautiful light oil which is delicious in salads, but it oxidises fast and goes rancid so it is best bought in small quantities. Renaissance artists favoured walnut oil for making paint.

SERVES 6

1 large lettuce, such as red oak leaf
250g Roquefort cheese, crumbled
90g whole walnuts
5 tablespoons Vinaigrette (see page 259) made with walnut oil
Small handful of chives, chopped

Separate, wash and dry the lettuce leaves and place them in a salad bowl. Add the crumbled Roquefort and the walnuts.

Just before serving, pour over the vinaigrette, toss the salad and sprinkle with chives.

pear and roquefort salad

The pear was one of Louis XIV's favourite fruits. La Quintinie, Louis' *Intendant Général des Jardins Fruitiers et Potagers de Toutes les Maisons Royales* (head gardener of fruits and vegetables) developed cultivars that ripened in varying weather conditions and recommended 47 varieties, including Cuisse-madame (my lady's thigh), that fruited for the court from July to February. Following the king's lead, there developed a great passion for fruit growing in France.

Pears, which should be eaten skin and all, are excellently set off by Roquefort cheese. The balsamic reduction gives an elegant syrupy tang to this recipe. Make it in advance, so that it cools before use. If the reduction has set too thick once it has cooled, thin it with a dash of boiling water. A balsamic reduction is handy to have in the fridge to add a contrasting burst of flavour to a tomato and buffalo mozzarella salad or some roast vegetables. The quantity given here makes a little more than is needed for this recipe – the rest will keep in a small sterilised jar (see page 273) in the fridge for a fortnight.

SERVES 6

150ml balsamic vinegar
1 tablespoon honey
250ml water
½ lemon
3 pears
75g rocket
1 handful of basil leaves
1 tablespoon best-quality olive oil
125g Roquefort cheese

Pour the balsamic vinegar into a nonreactive saucepan and bring to the boil. Immediately lower the heat so that the vinegar simmers gently and reduces by about a third. Add the honey and let the reduction bubble until it starts to become syrupy. This takes about 10 minutes and needs to be watched carefully in its final stages, as it can burn or reduce too far. Set it aside to cool, when it will thicken further.

Put the water into a bowl squeeze the juice from the lemon into it. Core the pears, slice thinly them and immediately submerge the slices in the lemony water to stop them oxidising and turning brown.

Dress the rocket and basil with the oil. Divide between 6 small plates and arrange the pear slices overlapping on top. Crumble the Roquefort on top of the pears. Finish with a drizzle of the balsamic reduction.

chicory, orange and walnut salad

My aunt very generously invited me to live with her for my first year at York University. She is famous within the family for her excellent cooking and I enjoyed many lively discussions about cookery and music over her Aga. She also had all the Elizabeth David books, which I read voraciously. My uncle, the University GP, grew magnificent vegetables on his allotment and, for the date, some unusual types, such as sea kale, salsify and Jerusalem artichokes alongside the good things of life such as artichokes and asparagus. (When the Amadeus string quartet, resident in the music department, came round for supper my aunt gave them artichoke soup; one of them quipped that she was the first person to turn them into a wind quartet!)

Below is recipe for one of my aunt's salads. My uncle grew the chicory. My grandfather (the father of my aunt) was another skilful domestic chicory grower and 'forced' them, under his bed, taking advantage of the warmth and dark.

SERVES 4

4 medium heads of chicory, about 450g in total
3 oranges
60g whole walnuts
½ quantity Vinaigrette (see page 259), made using
   3 tablespoons walnut oil in place of the olive oil

Trim the bases of the chicory heads and cut out the cores with a sharp and pointed knife. Place the leaves in a large salad bowl.

Peel the oranges, cut them in half and chop them roughly into half moons. Add them to the bowl with the chicory leaves. Scatter over the walnuts.

When you are ready to serve, add the dressing and toss the salad.

VARIATION

Add a handful of watercress, about 50g, to the chicory.

avocado and orange salad

This fresh and fruity salad is best made shortly before serving to avoid the avocado discolouring. If this is not possible, sprinkle the avocado with lemon juice as soon as you have cut it.

SERVES 4

3 medium oranges
2 avocados
3 tablespoons olive oil
1 tablespoon lemon juice
2 teaspoons honey
Salt and pepper
2 sprigs of mint, leaves picked and finely chopped

Peel the oranges and cut them crossways into 5mm-thick slices. Lay them in overlapping segments on a flat serving plate.

Remove the avocado stones, peel the fruit and slice vertically. Arrange on top of the orange slices.

Mix together the olive oil, lemon juice and honey and pour the dressing over the salad. Season and scatter the mint on top.

VARIATION

Serve on a bed of rocket, lamb's lettuce and/or watercress.

summer lunch
in the garden

A midsummer lunch with family and friends in the garden, when all the roses are out and the birds are singing, is heaven. If you have no courgette flowers for picking, some thin round slices of courgette make a good substitute. This lunch can be made after an impromptu decision earlier in the morning. Should you have vine or fig leaves, lay them on the plate under the cheese with their pointed leaves peeping out.

Courgette Flowers with Sage Leaves *page 52*

Large Mixed Salad *page 155*

Tortilla *page 54*

Puy Lentil Salad with Lemon,
Cumin and Herbs *page 170*

Plate of local cheeses *from the farmers' market*

Baked Peaches Stuffed with Almonds and Crushed
Cardamom Seeds served with crème fraîche *page 194*

TO DRINK

Chilled yellow-gold Alsatian Pinot Gris, maybe with
some *vin santo* to go with the baked peaches and
to round off the meal; home-made lemonade
with honey for the children

large mixed salad

A dazzling salad for a sunny Saturday lunch in the garden. Having set up a foundation of lettuce and grilled vegetables you can have a merry time creating a blaze of colour with heritage tomatoes: chartreuse Green Zebra, deep ruby *Coeur de Boeuf*, the dark and exotic but oh-so-sweet Russian *Noire de Crimée* and the blushing wild yellow *Ananas*.

The aim with the eggs is to catch the yolks whilst they are still a little gooey inside. The timing of this will depend on their size and freshness; if they are not really fresh, reduce the cooking time.

SERVES 8–10

1 aubergine, sliced vertically
2 red Romano peppers, sliced vertically
1 courgette, sliced vertically
2 tablespoons olive oil, plus extra for greasing
8 eggs
1 small red oak leaf lettuce
1kg tomatoes, sliced
16 black olives
60g pine nuts, toasted
1 quantity Vinaigrette (see page 259)
2 sprigs of parsley, leaves picked and chopped

Preheat the grill on a medium setting.

Spread the aubergine, romano pepper and courgette slices on an oiled baking tin and lightly brush the upper sides of the vegetables with oil. Grill until cooked, turning once; the aubergine and courgette should be lightly browned. (The peppers and courgette will take roughly 10 minutes to cook, while the aubergine will need about 15 minutes.)

Meanwhile, boil the eggs for 8 minutes. Immediately plunge the eggs into cold water with ice cubes to cool them, then remove the shells.

Spread the lettuce leaves over a large plate. Arrange the aubergines, courgettes and peppers on top. Lay the tomato slices over the vegetables. Cut the eggs vertically into quarters and lay these over the tomatoes.

Scatter the black olives and pine nuts over the top of the salad. Just prior to serving, pour over the vinaigrette and scatter over the chopped parsley.

raw baby artichokes with parmesan

Carpaccio di carciofi is one of the joys of spring. You need to find the tender small artichokes, such as *violette de Provence*, which come in bunches at the market. Artichokes oxidise and discolour very quickly once they are cut, so they need immediately to be put into the lemon juice to arrest this process.

SERVES 4

4 tablespoons lemon juice
6 baby artichokes
30g Parmesan cheese shavings
Salt and pepper

Put the lemon juice in a small dish.

Preparing 1 artichoke at a time, pull off the tough outer leaves to reveal the younger spring green leaves underneath. Chop off the spiky artichoke top and, using a potato peeler, peel the skin off the stem. Trim the stem to neaten. With either a knife or a mandoline, slice the artichoke thinly and immediately put the slices into the lemon juice. As you add subsequent artichoke slices, stir them around to ensure that the lemon juice coats them all.

Arrange the artichoke slices, overlapping one another, on a plate and pour over them a little of the remaining lemon juice. Lightly salt the artichokes. Place the Parmesan shavings on top and add a generous quantity of freshly ground pepper.

VARIATION

Sprinkle 1 tablespoon chopped parsley on the top.

grilled courgette salad

Lightly charred courgettes make a superb salad with a fragrant citrusy dressing of lemon, basil and mint; pine nuts add a subtle crunch. This dish is great as part of a refreshing trio of salads, alongside Raw Baby Artichokes with Parmesan (see page 156) and Avocado and Orange Salad (see page 153).

SERVES 4

4 small courgettes
3 tablespoons artisan olive oil
1 red chilli, deseeded and finely chopped
1 garlic clove, finely chopped
Salt and pepper
Grated zest and juice of ½ lemon
30g pine nuts, toasted
Handful of basil leaves, chopped
Handful of mint leaves, chopped

Using a mandoline, slice the courgettes lengthways into ribbons. Mix 1½ tablespoons of the olive oil with the chilli and garlic, season, and lightly brush the mixture over the courgettes.

Heat up a griddle pan over a medium heat and lightly char the courgettes, about 2 minutes on each side. Leave to cool.

Make a dressing with the remaining olive oil and the lemon zest and juice. When ready to serve, place the courgettes on a serving plate and pour the dressing over them. Sprinkle with pine nuts, basil and mint.

red cabbage and roasted sunflower seed salad

The ancient Egyptians, Greeks and Romans all cultivated cabbage with enthusiasm. In the sixteenth century, red cabbage was one of the first new varieties to be developed in Europe. In making this salad, see that you mix the cabbage as soon as possible with its acid dressing, as red cabbage discolours immediately once it is exposed to oxygen and turns mauve and blue. The acidic dressing prevents discolouration. This salad goes well with Falafel (see page 46).

SERVES 10 AS A SIDE DISH

100g sunflower seeds
150ml goats' yogurt
Grated zest and juice of ½ lemon
1 small red cabbage, about 550g
Handful of parsley, leaves picked and finely chopped

Toast the sunflower seeds until lightly browned, either shaking them in a dry frying pan for about 2 minutes or for about 4 minutes in the oven at 180°C.

Combine the yogurt and lemon juice and zest in a mixing bowl.

Remove the tough inner core of the cabbage and, using a mandoline, finely slice its leaves – the food processor slicer also does this well. Mix the leaves with the dressing quickly and add about three-quarters of the parsley. When you are ready to serve, add the toasted sunflower seeds, turn out the salad into a clean bowl and sprinkle the remaining parsley on top.

cauliflower and caper salad

Good-quality capers pair excellently with raw cauliflower in this salad. If you can find Romanesco and purple cauliflowers, mix florets from them with the standard white variety – the colouring becomes amazingly intense. When you shave the cauliflower florets, leave a bit of stalk on them to stop them disintegrating. This salad makes a great starter.

SERVES 6

1 small cauliflower (about 500–600g)
80g capers
6 tablespoons lemon juice
Handful of parsley, leaves picked and chopped
Salt and pepper
90g Pecorino cheese shavings

Remove the cauliflower stalk and, using a mandoline, finely shave the cauliflower florets and place them in a mixing bowl.

Add the capers, lemon juice and parsley to the bowl and mix together. Season with salt and pepper.

Place on a serving dish and add the Peccorino shavings, lightly mixing them into the cauliflower.

picnic

Off to the opera or a play with a long interval for a special picnic in the elegant garden of the venue, eaten on a picnic rug spread over the neatly cut grass. The pop of a Champagne cork heralds the start of the meal. In fact, we rarely drink real Champagne as there are so many superb sparkling white wines to tempt us 'made in the champagne style' from France and Catalonia at half the price. Catalan soup at garden temperature with zesty hints of orange opens the meal. The impressive-looking Spinach Roulade is remarkably amenable to travelling. Choose the best organic Parmesan to garnish the Raw Baby Artichokes. Lemon Tart with a dollop of whipped cream is a great treat for the end. The second part of the show is awaited with anticipation...

Catalan Fennel Soup *page 20*

Spinach Roulade with Tomato Sauce *page 132*

Jersey Royal new potatoes with Pesto *page 263*

Raw Baby Artichokes with Parmesan *page 156*

Lemon Tart with whipped cream *page 207*

TO DRINK

Sparkling Vouvray brut and a regal red Burgundy such as Beaune or Nuits St Georges

classic potato salad

Potato salad is a perennial favourite for parties. The mixture of freshly dug organic new potatoes, quails' eggs and French beans in mayonnaise is a winner. Remember, mayonnaise can be lightened by adding a small amount of water, but tread carefully here – I'm talking about by the teaspoon and half teaspoon.

This salad works well alongside Spinach Roulade (see page 132), Puy Lentil Salad with Lemon, Cumin and Herbs (see page 170) and Roquefort and Walnut Salad (see page 149).

SERVES 4

600g new potatoes, scrubbed
2 tablespoons olive oil
10 quails' eggs
150g French beans
Small handful of tarragon leaves, finely chopped
Small handful of chives, finely chopped
200g Mayonnaise (see page 256)
Salt and pepper

Gently boil the potatoes until tender, about 15 minutes. Drain well and cut each potato in half. Place the potatoes in salad bowl and toss them in the olive oil. Leave to cool.

Meanwhile, boil the quails' eggs in salted water for exactly 2 minutes. (A chip basket works well for lowering them in and out of the saucepan.) Plunge them into iced water, then shell when they are cold. Leave time for this manoeuvre: peeling quails eggs is famously fiddly. I find it helpful to tap and roll the egg on a chopping board until the eggs are crazed all over. Then start peeling at the rounded end – if you are lucky, the whole shell will peel off in a spiral. Failing this, try sliding a small implement between the white and the membrane and ease it gently away from the egg.

Steam the French beans until al dente, about 4 minutes. Add to the potatoes.

Throw the herbs over the potatoes and beans. Add the mayonnaise, season and mix thoroughly. Gently mix in the quails' eggs.

VARIATION

Substitute Pesto (see page 263) for the mayonnaise.

potato salad with crème fraîche

The Incas developed such a variety of potatoes that they measured their units of time by how long it took the different types to cook. It was Spanish ships that brought the potato to Europe from the New World but initially the Spanish Church and nobility scorned it as 'poor food' and potatoes were supplied to prisons, hospitals and the military. Indeed for much of the eighteenth century potatoes were positively banned in France as they were thought to cause leprosy, but after the pioneer nutritionist, Antoine-Augustin Parmentier (1737–1813) survived prison in Prussia, during the Seven Years' War, on a diet of the vegetable he promoted them strongly; Queen Marie Antoinette was to be seen with a bouquet of potato flowers in her hair. Thus dishes à *la Parmentier* celebrate the nutritious potato.

This potato salad can be knocked up in double-quick time and is my favourite for taking on an impromptu picnic. I love the crème fraîche with the tang of lemon zest and the crunch of the spring onions, which combine perfectly with the young potatoes.

SERVES 4

600g new potatoes
4 spring onions, finely chopped
150g crème fraîche
Grated zest and juice of ½ lemon
Salt and pepper
Handful of chives

Gently boil the potatoes until tender, about 15 minutes. Drain and leave to cool (if you have time).

Put the potatoes in a salad bowl and add the spring onions, crème fraîche and the lemon zest and juice. Season and, using a pair of scissors, chop the chives over the salad. Mix well and serve.

VARIATION

Add 200g drained canned artichokes, chopped in half.

ensaladilla rusa

This dish reminds me of living, while a student, in Toledo in Central Spain, where I first enjoyed it along with Tortilla (see page 54), olives laced with crumbled dried red chilli, and a small glass of red wine, in tiny but magical tapas bars. In the autumn the inhabitants dried their pointed red peppers by threading them on a string and hanging them from their windows – a beautiful sight against the warm stone. Once they were dried they could be added to almost anything or ground into paprika.

Come home with friends from a summer concert to an *Ensaladilla Rusa*, some Tuscan Spinach and Ricotta Gnudi (see page 116) and Chicory, Orange and Walnut Salad (see page 152).

SERVES 4

500g waxy potatoes
100g small carrots, peeled
100g French beans, chopped into 4cm lengths
100g freshly shelled peas
1 red pepper, chopped
45g stoned black olives, chopped
45g capers
2 teaspoons sweet paprika
2 teaspoons dill, chopped
2 tablespoons parsley, chopped
200g Aïoli (see page 256)
Salt and pepper

Boil the potatoes and carrots until soft, about 15 minutes. Drain and dice them and place in a mixing bowl.

Steam the beans until soft, about 5 minutes. Steam the peas until tender, about 2 minutes.

Save some of the vegetables for decoration. Put the rest of the beans, peas, red pepper, olives, capers, paprika and herbs with the potatoes and carrots in the mixing bowl. Add the aïoli and mix well. Season.

Shape the mixture into a mound on a large plate and decorate with the reserved vegetables.

carottes râpées

This dish was served as a starter the night I arrived in Paris to spend the year working on French Baroque music in the Bibliothèque Nationale. It is a well-loved salad found all over France that can be rustled up speedily but is always a delight.

SERVES 6

600g carrots, peeled and grated
Juice of 2 large lemons
2 tablespoons olive oil
2 tablespoons honey
Salt and pepper

Place the carrots in a salad bowl.

Mix the lemon juice, olive oil and honey together. Add them to the grated carrots. Season to taste with salt and plenty of freshly ground black pepper.

VARIATION

– Sprinkle 3 tablespoons dry-roasted sunflower seeds over the top.
– Substitute 200g raw beetroot for 200g of the carrots.
– Substitute 600g unpeeled raw courgettes for the carrots.

honeyed carrots

It has been suggested that the modern carrot finds its origins in Afghanistan and was introduced to the Eastern Mediterranean at the time of the Arab expansion between the eighth and the tenth centuries. The twelfth-century Andalusían agriculturalist Ibn al-Awam delighted in its juicy and tasty flavour. From thence, it travelled to France, Germany and the Netherlands in the fourteenth century and to Britain in the fifteenth. The first genuinely orange carrots appear in Dutch paintings in the seventeenth century; the orange comes from beta carotene which the human body converts into vitamin A. *Carottes Vichy*, as this recipe is known in France, was originally cooked in Vichy water, and eaten daily as part of the cure in the spa town of that name in the Auvergne.

SERVES 4

500g young carrots
45g butter
3 tablespoons honey
Salt and pepper
1 tablespoon chopped parsley

Leaving about 2cm of their tops attached, peel the carrots. Chop any large carrots in half lengthways.

Place the carrots, butter and honey in a large saucepan and cover with water. Bring to the boil and simmer until the carrots are almost cooked, about 15 minutes. Then boil vigorously to reduce the liquid to a shiny glaze.

Season and serve sprinkled with parsley.

puy lentil salad with lemon, cumin and herbs

I love the taste of Puy lentils brought to life by an abundance of herbs, fruity olive oil, a dash of lemon, cumin, Maldon salt and freshly ground black pepper. The luscious herbs remind me of an Iranian friend, Farad, who once produced an enormous bunch at a picnic for which we had all brought along a dish. He had grown them specially in the garden and we ate them, undressed, as a salad. Iranians eat huge quantities of herbs.

The fresh herbs here might include chives, coriander, cress, dill, mint, oregano, parsley, sorrel and tarragon – choose whatever looks most succulent and good.

SERVES 6–8

300g Puy lentils
100ml best-quality olive oil
Grated zest and juice of a lemon
1½ teaspoons cumin seeds
Salt and pepper
Large handful of parsley, leaves picked and chopped
Large handful of mixed fresh herbs, leaves picked and chopped

Overnight, or half a day before you cook them, put the lentils in a large bowl and generously cover them with boiling water.

When you are ready to cook, drain the lentils, then cook in fresh boiling water until tender, 15–40 minutes, depending on their age. Drain and place in a large salad bowl. Leave to cool.

When the lentils have cooled, add the olive oil and stir in thoroughly. Add the lemon zest and juice and the cumin seeds. Season. Finally, add plenty of herbs and mix in well.

french beans

The French bean was first domesticated over 5000 years ago in Central America. Its name, *phaseolus*, likens the pod to a small swift sailing boat. Prior to Columbus' discovery of America, Europeans relied on the broad bean – which goes back at least to the Bronze Age – for sustaining them through the winter. When the French bean arrived it quickly established itself as a favourite with European cooks and gardeners and had acquired its label as 'French' by 1572. Indeed, the French, attempting to distinguish it from the broad bean (*fève*), named it *haricot*, a corruption of the Aztec *ayacotl*.

As well as the slender green beans being delicious hot, they are excellent in salads. I love to serve French beans dripping with butter and garlic at a dinner party. I learnt this stress-free manner of cooking them from our neighbour Hélène in Marnaves, in France. Like this, one can easily cook French beans for 20.

SERVES 4

500g French beans
70g butter
4 garlic cloves, finely chopped
Salt and pepper

Steam the beans until al dente, about 4 minutes.

Gently melt the butter in a large frying pan (which has a lid) and remove it from the heat. Add the beans and garlic and cover.

Roughly 5 minutes before you are ready to serve them, fry the beans in the buttery garlic on a medium heat until they are well heated through, about 2 minutes. Season and dish up.

VARIATION

Substitute 500g purple-sprouting broccoli or calabrese for the beans.

leeks in red wine

The ancient Greeks and Romans had a penchant for leeks,
particularly the Emperor Nero, a passionate singer, who believed
they would improve his voice. He ate so many that his people
nicknamed him *Porrophagus* (leek-eater). The Welsh connection
is noted by seventeenth-century writer and gardener John Evelyn,
who commented positively in 1699: 'the Welch, who eat them much,
are observ'd to be very fruitful: they [the leeks] are also friendly
to the lungs and stomach'.

Leeks in red wine also make a delicious cold starter.

SERVES 6

1kg medium leeks
6 tablespoons olive oil
350ml red wine
120ml hot vegetable stock, made with
  ½ teaspoon Marigold bouillon powder
Pepper

Carefully clean the leeks and slice off most of their green tops.

Heat the oil in a large frying pan (which has a lid), place the leeks in it
side by side and fry, turning them over as they colour. When they are
coloured, add the wine and stock. Cover and simmer, turning the leeks
occasionally, until they are are soft, about 15 minutes.

Lay the leeks in a warmed, shallow serving dish. Boil the liquid to
reduce it down to roughly 170ml, about 3–5 minutes. Pour the
sauce over the leeks, grind the pepper over the top and serve hot.

VARIATION

Substitute the sticks of a large head of celery for the leeks.

catalan spinach

It was this recipe that first whetted my appetite to learn more about the marvels of Catalan cuisine. The French viol virtuoso, Christophe Coin, taught it to me many years ago, calling it Jordi's spinach, as he had learnt it from the Catalan virtuoso, Jordi Savall.

For me, the Catalan delight in using dried fruit and nuts, inherited from the Arabs, makes this manner of serving spinach irresistible. Both pine nuts and raisins were important Catalan exports in the Middle Ages. If you are lucky enough to find sweet golden sultanas for this recipe, all the better.

SERVES 4

750g spinach
4 tablespoons olive oil
3 garlic cloves, chopped
45g pine nuts
45g raisins
Salt and pepper

Thoroughly wash the spinach and drain. If the leaves are large, chop them roughly, trimming off any thick stems. Put the wet spinach in a large pot, cover and let it steam in the water clinging to its leaves until it is soft and wilted, 2–3 minutes. Take care at this stage not to let it dry out and scorch. Drain off any water that remains.

Heat the oil in a large frying pan and sauté the garlic and pine nuts over a low heat until they turn light gold, about 1–2 minutes. Add the spinach and raisins, season and fry on a medium heat until the dish is cooked through, about 5 minutes.

VARIATION

Use chard instead of spinach.

buttered chard

I love growing rainbow chard because it gives colour to the garden throughout the year. Even in winter it is valiantly producing leaves of varying greens and copper, with stalks of brilliant crimson, deep scarlet and shocking yellow. I also like growing it for its nutty flavour, which is enhanced by cooking the stalks as well. When I made this dish for a French friend, he enquired curiously what had I put into the chard as he could not recognise what had produced this flavour. I had to say that there was no magic ingredient, just the stalks and lots of butter. To which he replied: 'Ah yes: *mettre du beurre dans les épinards* (to put butter into spinach)' – a French idiom illustrating how adding something good can improve a difficult situation.

Use young tender leaves and stalks of around 20cm in total length for this recipe.

SERVES 4–6

500g chard
60g butter
Salt and pepper

Thoroughly wash the chard and dry. Tear the chard leaves from their stalks, roughly chop them and set them aside. Slice the stalks finely on the diagonal (this makes them less fibrous).

Heat the butter in a saucepan and fry the chard stalks gently until they are soft, about 10 minutes. Add the chopped leaves and continue to fry until the leaves are soft, about 5 minutes. Season and serve.

roasted or grilled peppers and aubergines

Escalivada is a favourite Catalan dish, to which I was introduced by my wonderful friend and Catalan neighbour, Montserrat. Montse is a passionate and highly gifted chef, who began her culinary story as a young girl, cooking for the family of fifteen under the watchful eye of her mother on her parents' farm in Barcelona province. The area supports many excellent artisan producers, small family businesses making superb cheese, wine, olive oil and the most delicious vinegar I have ever tasted. In 2012, Montse opened her own Catalan restaurant, La Cuina, in Cardiff and in less than a year she was mentioned in the *Michelin Guide*. For a sophisticated Catalan light bite, serve *escalivada* to accompany *calçots* with Romesco Sauce (see page 60).

SERVES 6

3 aubergines
4 Romano peppers
4 tablespoons artisan olive oil
2 tablespoons artisan vinegar
Maldon sea salt

Prick the aubergine skins in a few places to stop them bursting.

To roast the vegetables, preheat the oven to 180°C. Put the whole vegetables on an oven tray on a sheet of foil. Roast in the oven, turning them over occasionally, until they become black and blistered, about 45 minutes for the peppers and 1 hour for the aubergines.

Alternatively, to grill the vegetables, preheat the grill on a medium-high setting. Put the whole vegetables in a roasting tray quite close to the heat and grill, turning occasionally, until they are black and blistered, about 15 minutes for the peppers and 20–25 minutes for the aubergines.

Once the peppers are cooked, put them in an empty pan with its lid on until they are cool enough to handle, about 10 minutes, to loosen their skins. Peel the peppers, removing the stalk and seeds. Reserve the juices.

When the aubergines are cooked and slightly cooled, make a lengthways incision from the top to the bottom and gently scoop out the flesh from the burnt skin.

Cut the pepper and aubergine flesh into vertical strips and lay them out prettily, alternating the pepper (with its reserved juices) and the aubergine. Sprinkle with the olive oil and vinegar and a little sea salt.

roast jerusalem artichokes

The Jerusalem artichoke came to Europe from North America, where it was eaten by the native Americans. Samuel de Champlain, who founded Quebec, described them in 1605 as 'roots which they [the native Americans] cultivate... with the taste of artichokes'. It is a member of the sunflower family and, like the sunflower, has flowers that follow the sun, a *girasol* – of which 'Jerusalem' is believed to be a corruption. In France it is called *topinambour* after six Brazilians from the Topinambous tribe who provoked great curiosity when they were brought back to Paris in 1613, about the same time as the arrival of the Jerusalem artichoke or Canadian truffle, as it was first called.

Jerusalem artichokes are very easy to grow in the garden. Several plants produce an abundant crop of tubers, with minimal attention, and will repeat their performance indefinitely.

When roasted, Jerusalem artichokes are excellent warm in salads with goats' cheese and young salad leaves. They also make a fine salad on their own, raw, sliced paper thin with a mandoline and dressed with some lemon, honey and a little olive oil.

Serve this dish with a squeeze of lemon or, if you are feeling extravagant, some Hollandaise Sauce (see page 257).

SERVES 4

350g Jerusalem artichokes
2 garlic cloves, chopped
4 sprigs of thyme
2 tablespoons olive oil
Salt and pepper

Preheat the oven to 180°C.

Scrub the artichokes thoroughly, getting any grit out of the nooks and crannies of their nobbles. Slice them in half lengthways and put them in a bowl with the garlic, thyme sprigs and olive oil and mix well. Place the artichokes in a single layer, so that they can brown, face down in a baking tray with the garlic and sprigs of thyme. Season.

Roast the artichokes, turning them after 15 minutes, until they are just tender and their skins are crispy, about 30 minutes. Be careful not to overcook them. Serve immediately.

baked beetroot

Small beetroots are the tastiest choice for this recipe. Beetroot has great potential for adding to salads – it goes well with rocket, watercress, chicory, orange, apple, lentils and goats' cheese.

SERVES 6, WITH SOME LEFT OVER FOR A SALAD

1 kg beetroot
1 orange
1 garlic bulb
2 bay leaves
3 sprigs of thyme
2 tablespoons olive oil, plus extra oil to rub
   on the beetroots
Salt and pepper
1 tablespoon finely chopped parsley
Butter, cream or olive oil, to serve (see below)

Preheat the oven to 200°C.

Wash the beetroots thoroughly, trying not to damage their skins, and trim the stems down to 5cm, leaving the roots alone. Leaving the roots and stem intact in this way ensures that the sweet juices do not bleed out. Rub the beetroots in oil – this makes them easier to peel when they are cooked. Put them on a large roasting tin with plenty of space between them.

Avoiding the pith, pare the rind off the orange, then cut the orange in half and juice it.

Add the garlic bulb, bay leaves, thyme sprigs, the orange peel and juice and the olive oil to the beetroot. Fill the roasting tin 3cm deep with water (or deeper if the beetroots are large) and cover it with foil, crimping it around the edges of the roasting tin to keep the moisture in and prevent the beetroots drying out whilst cooking.

Bake until the beetroots are soft enough to slide a knife into, about 1 hour for small beetroots and up to 2 hours or more if they are large. Immediately place the beetroots in a saucepan with a lid to help steam off their skins. As soon as you can handle them, rub off the skins.

Put the beetroots in a serving dish, season and garnish with parsley.

Serve hot or cold, with some butter and perhaps a dash of cream if you are serving them hot or with olive oil drizzled over them if cold.

roast crown prince

It is known that pumpkins were grown in a Parisian kitchen garden on the Île de la Cité in the fourteenth century as they are described in a fascinating manuscript entitled *Le Ménagier de Paris*. By the seventeenth century the pumpkin has found its way into folktale and is playing a magical role in Perrault's tale of Cinderella.

In the autumn you can find piles of pumpkins with different coloured skins – mottled, streaked and spotted – at the farmers' markets that have so wonderfully come into our lives. I adore the rich autumnal flavour of roast Crown Prince, but if I am unable to find this variety I look for another orange-fleshed type with a low water content – that is to say not the traditional Halloween pumpkin, which is very watery, but perhaps a butternut squash.

If you are a forager or what my son Alex calls 'minted' you can lift this recipe to another level by using wild mushrooms. In fact, they are now available imported from Eastern Europe at an affordable price. Or mix chestnut mushrooms with some dried (and soaked) ceps, which impart a heady, rich and exotic flavour.

SERVES 6–8

1kg slice of Crown Prince pumpkin, deseeded
2 tablespoons olive oil
2 red chillies, deseeded and sliced
1 whole garlic bulb, unpeeled
1 sprig of sage, leaves picked and roughly chopped
Salt and pepper
400g mushrooms, trimmed and sliced

Preheat the oven to 200°C.

Slice the unpeeled pumpkin, coat the pieces with the oil and spread them out on a large baking tray so that they do not overlap. Add the chilli, whole cloves of garlic in their skins and the sage leaves. Season. Roast for 20 minutes.

Turn the pumpkin slices and add the mushrooms, tossing them in the oil that is already in the baking tray. The dish is cooked when the pumpkin is golden and soft and the mushrooms are browned, about 10 minutes. Serve hot.

gratin dauphinois

This recipe helped Alex put *Wales on the Menu* (see page 108). He showed his Welsh colours by using Gwynt y Ddraig cider.

SERVES 6 (AS A SIDE DISH AND 4 AS A MAIN DISH)

Butter, for greasing
400ml organic cider
250ml cream
1kg waxy potatoes, sliced thinly with a mandoline
1 large onion, finely chopped
4 garlic cloves, finely chopped
4 bay leaves
Nutmeg
Salt and pepper

Preheat the oven to 210°C. Butter a large shallow (6cm deep) earthenware baking dish.

Mix together the cider and cream in a jug.

Spread a third of the potato slices in the bottom of the prepared dish, scatter over half the chopped onion and garlic and bay leaves and season with a grating of nutmeg and salt and pepper, to taste. Sprinkle with a liberal coating of the cider and cream. Repeat the layering process using half the remaining potato slices and all the remaining onions, garlic and bay leaves. Season and sprinkle over some cider and cream. Finish with a layer of the remaining potatoes, season and pour over the rest of the cider and cream. Cover the dish with buttered kitchen foil, bending it over the edges of the dish.

Bake until the potatoes are cooked through and begin to caramelise, about 1½ hours, then remove the foil and cook until the potatoes are golden and crisp, about 15 minutes.

VARIATIONS

– If cooking *dauphinois* as a main dish, you might like to add 100g Parmesan cheese, grated, on top or 200g Taleggio, sliced. Add the cheese for the last 5 minutes of the cooking time.
– If you are fortunate enough to have ceps growing in your local woods, add 750g to the potatoes, or use 600g chestnut mushrooms with 50g dried ceps. (Cover the dried ceps with boiling water and soak for 10 minutes. Mix the reconstituted ceps with the chestnut mushrooms and potatoes. Strain the soaking water and add to the cider and cream.)

moroccan saffron potatoes

I find I can buy good-quality Spanish saffron at a very reasonable price from our local Indian and Middle Eastern shops. In this version of saffron potatoes I particularly like the way the freshness of the celery enlivens the potatoes, an idea I have borrowed from the talented food writer Nadine Abensur. The dish is ready when the potatoes are meltingly soft and covered with a sticky, translucent sauce oozing flavour – a fabulous warming supper dish.

SERVES 6 (AS A SIDE DISH AND 4 AS A MAIN DISH)

100ml olive oil
2 large red onions, finely chopped
5 garlic cloves, finely chopped
2 green chillies, finely chopped
1kg medium waxy potatoes, cut in half lengthways
2 generous pinches of saffron, infused in 100ml hot water
½ head of celery, chopped
60g raisins
Salt and pepper
Handful of coriander, leaves picked and roughly chopped

In a large saucepan, heat the olive oil over a medium-low heat and fry the onions until soft and golden, about 10 minutes. Add the garlic and chillies and fry for a couple of minutes, then mix in the potatoes and fry for another couple of minutes. Add the saffron water and simmer with a lid on the pan for about 25 minutes until the potatoes begin to soften.

Stir in the celery and continue to cook with the lid off. If the sauce becomes too dry add a couple of tablespoons more water. When the potatoes have nearly cooked, add the raisins and season. Simmer for a further 10 minutes to let the sweetness of the raisins infuse the sauce.

Serve hot with coriander scattered on top.

VARIATION

Add 2 bulbs of fennel, each cut into 6 wedges, at the same time as you add the potatoes.

provençal herby potatoes

Broadly speaking, potatoes fall into two categories: floury and waxy.
Floury potatoes disintegrate when boiled, while waxy ones hold their
shape. Choose your potato to suit your dish: floury for mashing and
baking and waxy for boiling, as in this traditional Provençal recipe
from Claudia Roden's *Invitation to Mediterranean Cooking*. Serve this
dish with the herbs and garlic and your very best artisan olive oil.

SERVES 6

1kg small waxy new potatoes, scrubbed
2 garlic bulbs, cut in half horizontally
4 bay leaves
4 sprigs of thyme
Salt and pepper
Best olive oil

Cover the potatoes with water in a pan, along with the garlic, bay
leaves and thyme. Bring to the boil, then simmer until soft. Leave
them in their water until you are ready to serve to absorb the flavours.
Drain, season and serve with a good splash of your favourite olive oil.

mashed potatoes with
olive oil, garlic and parsley

Garlic, olive oil and parsley are an excellent combination, which
marries delightfully with potatoes.

SERVES 6

1kg floury potatoes
120ml olive oil
4 garlic cloves, finely chopped
Salt and pepper
2 tablespoons chopped parsley

Boil the potatoes until soft. Drain, saving about 100ml of the cooking
water. Mash the potatoes with the olive oil and garlic, adding sufficient
cooking water to give them a soft texture. Season, mix in the parsley
and serve.

new potatoes, rocket and avocado, with a yogurt and horseradish dressing

Potatoes and horseradish are good companions. My son Alex created this recipe for us one summer's evening. Seventeenth-century writer and gardener John Evelyn considered horseradish as 'an excellent and universal condiment'; for the winter he recommended 'thin shavings mingled with our cold herbs'.

When I was small, my parents shared a beautiful Regency farmhouse in Norfolk with a retired couple, where we went for our holidays. The wife was a fantastic horsewoman and I would spend many hours with her in the kitchen as she cooked, hearing stories of her childhood, being brought up on a farm in Devonshire. She was a fine gardener, too, and horseradish was always grown on the dung heap, where it happily looked after itself. Horseradish is notorious for its invasive behaviour, so the dung heap was a good spot for it.

SERVES 4

500g new potatoes
Juice of 1 lemon
2 tablespoons grated horseradish
150ml yogurt
1 large shallot, finely sliced
2 small avocados
45g rocket
Salt and pepper

Boil the potatoes until soft. Drain.

Meanwhile, make the dressing. Mix together 1 tablespoon of the lemon juice, the horseradish, yogurt and shallot. Peel and slice the avocados and sprinkle with the remaining lemon juice.

Place the warm potatoes in a serving bowl. If they have collapsed a bit that is all the better for absorbing the feisty horseradish dressing. Toss in the rocket and avocado slices and lightly mix. Cover with the dressing, season and serve.

VARIATION

Substitute soured cream for the yogurt.

rösti

This is food designed for hardworking Swiss farmers and is absolutely delicious. Our Swiss friend, Ursula, recounts how her grandparents would have rösti with coffee for breakfast, then rösti with coffee again for supper – and they lived into their 90s. It is typical to serve rösti with some fine cheeses, such as artisan Gruyère or Reblochon, or some ripe goats' cheese with salad – the Chicory, Orange and Walnut Salad (see page 152) would be a good choice. Try Grilled Beetroot with Asparagus and Halloumi (see page 59) with rösti, or fresh Ezme (see page 38), or some Marinated Halloumi Kebabs (see page 83).

Rösti mit spiegelei (see the variation below) makes a satisfying brunch; I like to poach my eggs (see page 57) rather than fry them. Tasty Grilled Goats' Cheese Salad with Honey (see page 148) completes the meal.

MAKES 8 PANCAKES

700g waxy potatoes, skins on
90g butter
160g shallots or onions, finely chopped
Salt and pepper
2 tablespoons olive oil

Parboil the potatoes until barely cooked. Leave to cool, then grate them.

Meanwhile, heat the butter in a saucepan and soften the shallots over a medium-low heat, about 10 minutes. Mix the grated potatoes and buttery shallots in a bowl. Season.

Heat 1 tablespoon of the olive oil in a 26cm frying pan over a high heat. Divide the rösti mixture into 8 mounds. Place 4 of these in the frying pan and flatten them out with a spatula; they should be roughly 10cm in diameter. Fry until the undersides have formed a crispy crust (which holds the rösti together), 2–3 minutes. Reduce the heat to medium-low and fry for a further 5 minutes to cook through. Increase the heat to high, turn the rösti over and fry on the second side until the crispy and golden crust has formed, 2–3 minutes. Again, reduce the heat to medium-low to complete cooking, about 5 minutes. Keep this first batch warm in an oven set to 100°C while you fry the remaining batch in the same way. Serve 2 rösti per person immediately.

VARIATIONS

– Add 2 teaspoons finely chopped rosemary to the shallots.
– For traditional *rösti mit speigelei*, add a fried egg on top.

kasha

Kasha, which is made from roasted wholegrain buckwheat, is a staple food in Eastern Europe and Russia. If the buckwheat is not roasted, dry-roast it in a stainless steel frying pan. This both makes the taste nuttier and stops it from going mushy when it is cooked. Allow 50g buckwheat per person and cook it in one and half times its weight in water, that is to say 75ml water per 50g buckwheat. It can be served with a dollop of soured cream (called *smetana* in Eastern Europe) or with fried onion and wild mushrooms – or chestnut mushrooms with some dried ceps or chanterelles. Or serve it to accompany Mushroom Stroganoff (see page 92) and experiment with providing it with other recipes, such as Marinated Halloumi Kebabs (see page 83) or Sweet and Sour Tofu with Oyster Mushrooms (see page 94).

SERVES 4

300ml water
200g roasted buckwheat
Salt
30g butter

Bring the water to the boil. Stir in the buckwheat, put on a lid and simmer on a very low heat until the buckwheat is tender and the water is absorbed, about 8 minutes. Season it lightly with salt and stir in the butter, letting it melt in the heat of the kasha.

mushrooms in cream

In his book *A Journey to Paris in the Year 1698*, the natural historian
Dr Martin Lister, having first discussed all the vegetables eaten in Paris
at that date and noted how much the Parisians enjoyed asparagus and
sorrel, writes 'the French delight in nothing so much as *Mushroomes*,
of which they have daily, and all the Winter long, store[d] fresh and
new gathered in the Markets'. This year-round enjoyment, evidently
unknown to Lister in Britain, was due to the use of 'hot beds' created
from trenches of horse dung over which was strewn insulating straw.
In the nineteenth century the Parisians discovered that their disused
quarries, the stone from which had been used to build Paris, provided
the perfect steady temperature for the cultivation of mushrooms all
year round. The white button mushrooms that they grew became the
celebrated *champignons de Paris*.

This recipe is amazingly simple and absolutely delicious; it is one of
my mother's. I often serve it with Spinach Roulade (see page 132).

SERVES 6

600g white button mushrooms
225ml cream
2 bay leaves
Nutmeg
Salt and pepper

Preheat the oven to 180°C.

Put the mushrooms, cream and bay leaves in a casserole dish and
season with a grating of nutmeg and salt and pepper to taste. Bake,
covered, until the mushrooms are cooked and have flavoured the
cream, about 1 hour. Serve immediately.

DESSERTS

white peach, plum and blackberry crumble

This is a delightful summer crumble if you find yourself in the Mediterranean, where you can obtain fragrant white peaches, blackberries in the hedgerows and the little wild purple plums with an intense sunny flavour known as *prunes de cochon*. The name translates as pig's plums, and they are so named because they are so abundant that they were frequently fed to the family pig. *Prunes de cochon* grow wild by the roadside and three people can gather them easily by holding a large groundsheet under the tree and shaking the branches. Serve this crumble hot or cold, with cream.

SERVES 6

125g ground almonds
125g potato flour
125g honey
125g butter, softened, a further 30g for
   dotting, chopped, plus extra for greasing
6 white peaches
12 small purple plums
250g blackberries
Grated zest and juice of ½ lemon
60g flaked almonds

Preheat the oven to 170°C. Butter a 26cm ovenproof dish.

To make the crumble, combine the ground almonds, potato flour, honey and butter in a food processor.

Skin the peaches – put them in a bowl or jug, pour boiling water on them and leaving them to sit for about 30 seconds, then rub off the skins. Cut around the centres of the skinned peaches, remove the stones and slice the flesh. Cut the little plums in half and remove the stones. Lay the peaches, plums and blackberries in the prepared dish. Pour over the lemon juice and rind, then dot with the chopped butter. If the fruit is unripe, you could trickle over a little honey. Cover the fruit with the crumble and scatter the flaked almonds over the top.

Bake until the top is nicely coloured, about 30 minutes.

VARIATION

Make a crumble with 900g of your favourite fruits in place of the plums (try apricots, or apple and blackberries, or just blackberries).

poached peaches

White peaches send a wicked shiver of delight through me. As children at my grandparents' house, whilst the adults were having dinner, we would steal down across the bridge over the lake to the walled garden and help ourselves to beautiful white peaches, fresh and warm off the trees.

This dish is a boon for parties because it can be prepared in advance and, at the critical moment, warmed up. If you have fresh lavender in your garden, just before serving, sprinkle over a few lavender flowers, crushed between your fingers. You could even add a few rose petals.

SERVES 6

9 white peaches
Juice of 1 lemon
3 tablespoons fragrant honey
3 tablespoons Cointreau or dessert wine
3 lavender flowers

Skin the peaches – put them in a bowl or jug, pour boiling water on them and leaving them to sit for about 30 seconds, then rub off the skins. Cut around the centres of the skinned peaches, remove the stones and slice the flesh. Put the slices into a large frying pan. Mix in the lemon juice thoroughly, then the honey and Cointreau. Cover with a lid.

Roughly 10 minutes before you are ready to serve, gently warm the peaches through, turning them from time to time to coat them evenly in the honey and Cointreau. Crumble over the lavender flowers. Transfer the poached peach slices to serving bowls.

baked peaches stuffed with almonds and crushed cardamom seeds

These soft, warm and aromatic stuffed peaches make a lovely quick dessert served with crème fraîche that has long been a family favourite.

SERVES 6

6 peaches
120g blanched almonds, coarsely ground
3 tablespoons fragrant honey
1 egg yolk
30g butter, plus extra for greasing
Grated zest of 1 small orange
1 teaspoon cardamom seeds, crushed

Preheat the oven to 160°C. Lightly butter an ovenproof dish.

Cut the peaches in half. Remove the stones and a little of the flesh around the stones to create a larger cavity to stuff. Put the scooped-out flesh in a bowl and mix in the almonds, honey, egg yolk, butter, orange zest and cardamom seeds. Stuff the peaches with this mixture, spreading it over the cavity in each peach half in a little mound. Place the stuffed peach halves on the prepared ovenproof dish.

Bake until golden, about 30 minutes. Serve immediately.

cherry clafoutis

Clafoutis is a speciality of the Limousin region of France; its name comes from the Occitan *clafir* meaning 'to fill'. It was traditionally baked using the first red cherries of the season. There is also a custom of leaving the stones in, both to give the custard a better flavour and to prevent cherry juice mingling in with it. But do warn your guests that this dessert contains cherry stones!

SERVES 6

Butter, for greasing
500g cherries
4 eggs
100g fragrant honey
1 tablespoon potato flour, sieved
3 drops of vanilla essence
3 tablespoons cognac or Calvados
100ml cream
150ml milk
Maple sugar (optional)

Preheat the oven to 170°C. Butter a 22cm baking dish.

Wash and dry the cherries. Place them in the prepared baking dish.

In a food processor, combine the eggs, honey and potato flour. Add the vanilla and cognac and gradually add the cream and milk.

Pour the custard over the cherries and bake until the *clafoutis* forms a pale, golden crust and the cream has set, about 30 minutes.

Dust with maple sugar, if you wish, and serve warm.

VARIATIONS

Substitute apricots, plums (halved and stoned) or blackberries, blueberries and/or raspberries for the cherries.

catalan pears poached in honey, saffron and vanilla

Serve these elegant pears infused with a honey and saffron syrup with Macaroons (see page 251) or Vanilla Ice Cream (see page 221). Sixteenth-century herbalist John Gerarde professes that saffron 'is good for the head, and maketh the sences more quicke and lively, shaketh off heavy and drowsie sleepe, and maketh man merry'.

SERVES 8

8 pears, slightly underripe
Squeeze of lemon juice
700ml water
250g honey
2 generous pinches of saffron
2 teaspoons vanilla essence

Peel the pears but leave their stalks attached. Immerse the peeled pears in a bowl of water with a good squeeze of lemon juice in it, to stop them discolouring.

Bring the water, honey, saffron and vanilla to the boil in a pan that is large enough to take the 8 pears. Add the pears and bring the syrup back to the boil. Place some crumpled-up greaseproof paper over the pears to keep them submerged in the liquid. Reduce the heat and simmer until the pears are soft throughout, 30 minutes to 1 hour, depending on the ripeness of the pears. Pierce the pears with a fine skewer to check how soft they are.

Remove the pears from the liquid using a slotted spoon and place them in a serving bowl. Set aside.

Boil the liquid to reduce it to a thin, sweet syrup, about 15 minutes. Pour the syrup over the pears in the serving bowl. Set aside at room temperature for several hours before serving to allow the pears to be further infused by the syrup. This dish can profitably be made the day before serving, giving the the saffron and vanilla more time to infuse the pears.

baked quince

It is believed that the three 'golden apples' of the Hesperides that
Heracles stole for his eleventh labour were really quinces and that,
likewise, a quince was the golden 'apple' that Paris bestowed upon
Aphrodite – appropriately, a symbol of love, marriage and fertility.

In April in Marnaves, where we have a home, the hedgerows are
full of delicate white quince flowers fluttering in the breeze, a promise
of coming warmth.

According to Jane Grigson, baked quince was Sir Isaac Newton's
favourite pudding. The core and pips of the quince are naturally full
of pectin and help to make a delicious sauce. Serve the baked quince
hot with a dollop of thick whipped cream.

SERVES 4

2 large quinces
Grated zest and juice of 1 large lemon
300g fragrant honey
300ml water
1 vanilla pod, split in half lengthways

Heat the oven to 170°C.

Rub the grey fur off the skin of the quinces. With a large, strong knife,
cut each quince in half through the core. Do not remove the core, pips,
calyx or skin. Place the halved quinces in a baking dish, pour the lemon
juice and zest over them, then roll them around in the juice.

Put the honey, water and vanilla pod into a pan and dissolve the honey
in the water over a moderate heat. Arrange the quinces in the baking
dish so that their cut sides are facing up, then pour the honey syrup
over them. Cover the baking dish with kitchen foil and bake for 1 hour.

Reduce the heat to 150°C. Remove the foil from the baking dish, turn
the quinces in the syrup and, once again, arrange them so that the cut
sides face upwards. Bake until the quinces are tender and the juice has
become thick and syrupy, and the quinces have turned a magnificent
glossy red. The cooking time will depend on the quinces, but have
a look after half an hour. Serve immediately.

provençal apricot and almond pudding

Apricots and almonds are natural partners. When apricots are in their prime, I love to make this recipe, which comes originally from Claudia Roden's *An Invitation to Mediterranean Cooking*. Serve this pudding with a bowl of whipped cream.

SERVES 6

3 large eggs
100g butter, softened, plus extra for greasing
175g fragrant honey
1 teaspoon vanilla essence
150g blanched almonds, coarsely ground
1kg apricots, halved and stoned

SAUCE

80g honey
3 tablespoons water
250g apricots, stoned and cut in quarters
2 tablespoons lemon juice
2 tablespoons Kirsch

Preheat the oven to 170°C. Butter a 30cm earthenware dish.

Blend the eggs, butter, honey and vanilla essence in a food processor. Add the almonds and continue blending until you have a soft cream. Pour the mixture into the prepared dish.

Place the apricot halves on top of the almond paste with their cut sides facing down and push them into the paste. Bake until the pudding is lightly coloured and set, about 45 minutes. Leave to cool.

To make the sauce, put the honey and water in a saucepan set over a medium heat and warm until you have a syrup. Add the apricots and lemon juice and simmer until the apricots are tender, about 10 minutes. Purée to a sauce with a hand-held blender. Leave to cool, then stir in the Kirsch.

Serve the apricot and almond pudding at room temperature with the cooled sauce.

fondant glacé chocolat et noix

A delicious chocolate cake, more along the lines of a gigantic chocolate sweet, which is easy to make, and freezes and keeps well. The use of the best chocolate that you can find is extremely important; I favour a chocolate with 70 per cent cocoa solids that is not too strong. If the flavour is too overpowering for your taste, mellow it by replacing 45g of the 70 per cent cocoa chocolate with the same amount of milk chocolate. And if you can lay your hands on succulent *prunes d'Agen* from South-West France, all the better.

SERVES 12

225g plain chocolate, split into pieces
175g butter
100g Brazil nuts
100g cashews
100g almonds
1 egg
100g prunes, stoned and chopped

Preheat the oven to 180°C. Line a 900g bread tin with baking parchment.

Melt the chocolate and butter together, either in a bowl in a microwave oven on a low setting, or in a bowl set over a saucepan of gently simmering water.

Meanwhile, place the nuts on a baking tray and roast in the oven for 8 minutes.

Beat the egg well and stir it into the melted chocolate. Add the nuts and prunes. Pour the mixture into the prepared bread tin and refrigerate overnight to set.

Turn the cake out of the bread tin and remove the baking parchment. Keep refrigerated until ready to serve. Slice thinly with a heavy and sharp knife.

plums in spicy red wine

I enjoy serving these *prunes aux épices* with *fondant glacé*, which, together, make a delicious and easy dessert. On other occasions I pair them with vanilla or ginger ice cream. A good Italian or Spanish wine works beautifully in this dish.

SERVES 6

750g red or purple plums, such as Victoria, halved and stoned
225ml red wine
1 large cinnamon stick
3 cloves
2 star anise
¼ teaspoon cardamom seeds, ground using a pestle and mortar
2 bay leaves
150g fragrant honey

Preheat the oven to 150°C.

Place the plum halves, cut sides facing down, on a 28cm × 18cm baking dish so that they cover the entire surface of the dish.

Put the wine, cinnamon stick, cloves, star anise, ground cardamom, bay leaves and honey in a saucepan and bring to the boil. Immediately pour the mixture over the plums and cover the dish with kitchen foil. Bake until the plums are soft, about 20 minutes, depending on the ripeness of the plums.

Serve either hot or cold.

VARIATIONS

– Put the hot plums and spicy wine straight into a sterilised bottling jar and boil in a water bath (see page 273). Once bottled, let them infuse for several weeks before using. Store for up to 1 year.
– Experiment with spices by substituting 2 teaspoons coriander seeds, 1 teaspoon green peppercorns and the grated zest of 1 orange and 1 lemon for the star anise, cardamom seeds and bay leaves (but retaining the cinnamon and cloves).

lemon tart

It was the Arabs who brought lemons to southern Europe, along with so many other good things. Ibn Jamiya (the eleventh-century physician of Saladin, the sultan of Egypt and Syria) wrote a *Treatise of the Lemon*, including recipes, which was translated into Latin and published in Venice in 1583.

Tarte au citron is a classic and a perennial favourite. After a trip to the dentist as kids we always went to Sagne in Marylebone High Street, for a sticky cake as a reward. What a place, with its chandeliers and evocative murals transporting you to exotic climes. I always chose a little personal *tarte au citron*, with 'citron' delicately piped on top in chocolate. I find the deep velvetiness of the lemon custard irresistible.

For 8 people use a 24cm tart dish and two-thirds the quantities.

SERVES 10–12

Butter, for greasing
1 quantity Sweet Tart Crust (see page 277)

LEMON CREAM
Grated zest and juice of 5–6 lemons (you need 200ml juice)
9 eggs
10 heaped tablespoons mild honey
250ml cream

Preheat the oven to 170°C. Butter a 28cm tart dish.

Make the sweet tart crust following the instructions on page 277. Press the crust thinly into the prepared tart dish so that it reaches half way up the sides of the dish. Bake until the crust is lightly browned, about 10 minutes. Remove from the oven. If the crust sides have collapsed, press them back into shape. Reduce the oven temperature to 130°C.

To make the lemon cream, blend together the lemon zest and juice, eggs and honey using a hand-held blender, then blend in the cream. Transfer the mixture to a saucepan and, being careful not to allow it to scramble, warm the lemon cream gently. Alternatively, put the bowl in a microwave oven and cook on a low setting for about 3 minutes. This process of warming up the cream before pouring it into the tart crust speeds up the cooking time of the tart.

Pour the warm mixture into the tart crust and cook until barely set, 15–20 minutes. Remove from the oven and leave to cool and continue setting for half an hour.

apple tart

French patisserie chefs have long possessed a most ingenious machine (see pages 210–11) that peels, cores and slices their apples in a trice for the classic *Tarte aux Pommes*. The baker in Marnaves makes *tartes aux pommes* to feed the whole village at the time of the summer *fêtes*; his special characteristic is his generous use of vanilla. Flavoursome traditional English or French eating apples give the best results for this tart. Given a choice, I would select a Cox's Orange Pippin. Serve this tart hot or cold, perhaps with a dollop of cream.

SERVES 8

Butter, for greasing
1 quantity Sweet Tart Crust (see page 277) made with 60g mild honey
  instead of 120g

FOR THE FILLING

300ml cream
2 eggs
60g fragrant honey, melted
2 teaspoons vanilla essence
8–10 Cox's Orange Pippin, Russet or Braeburn apples

Preheat the oven to 170°C. Butter a 38cm × 28cm baking tray.

Make the tart crust following the instructions on page 277. Press the pastry dough thinly into the prepared baking tray. Bake until the pastry is lightly browned, about 10 minutes.

Meanwhile, prepare the custard. Blend together the cream, eggs, honey and vanilla essence in a food processor.

Core the apples, cut them in half and slice thinly into half moons. Arrange the slices in neat overlapping lines on the pastry. Cover with the custard and bake until the apples are cooked and the custard has set, about 30 minutes.

moroccan oranges

For seventeenth-century writer and gardener John Evelyn, the orange 'sharpens the appetite [and] exceedingly refreshes'. I agree with him and I have a very soft spot for these honeyed oranges. The orange originally came from China. It was described in an Indian medical treatise, *Charaka Samhita*, around AD 100, and its modern Indian name of *naranga* is thought to have been derived from the Sanskrit *narunga*, meaning 'fruit like elephants'. Initially, it was the bitter Seville orange that travelled to southern Europe, but the sweet orange was known by the late fifteenth century. The clementine (whose arrival gives us such joy in the autumn and which makes a delightful decoration, perched in a line along the mantelpiece for Christmas) is a cross between the mandarin and the bitter Seville, bred by the priest Père Clément around 1900 in Algeria.

When the British Council took me to Morocco to play with a classical Moroccan group one March, there were bowlfuls of orange flowers for sale in the markets, smelling divine. The fresh oranges were often served peeled and cut into slices, sprinkled with orange flower water and cinnamon. I often serve this refreshing fruit salad at the end of a meal, sometimes with a little liquid honey, too.

These honeyed Moroccan oranges keep well in the fridge and are scrumptious served with thick cream.

SERVES 8

500g oranges
250g honey

Cut the oranges into thin slices, about 5mm thick. Put the slices in a pan in layers, adding honey to each layer. Cover with water. Place a good-fitting lid on the pan and simmer gently until the oranges are soft and the pith has become translucent, about 2 hours.

Remove the oranges with a slotted spoon and place in a bowl. Reduce the syrup until it starts to thicken and there is just the right amount of syrup to cover the oranges. (If you overstep the mark you can always add a couple of tablespoons of water.)

mince pies

Mince pies are a must for Christmas but finding a neutral-tasting, grain-free pastry that holds together to encase the home-made mincemeat is a challenge. Making the dough in the food processor has the advantage of it not being affected by the warmth of one's hands, but the time-honoured method of cutting and then rubbing the fat into the flour is a sound alternative.

MAKES 10–12 MINCE PIES

100g chickpea flour
100g potato flour, plus extra for dusting
100g butter, plus extra for greasing
2 tablespoons honey
250g Mincemeat (see page 265)
1 egg, beaten

Blend the chickpea flour and the potato flour with the butter in a food processor until you have fine crumbs. Add the honey and process to create a dough, adding a small amount of water as necessary. Put the dough in a plastic bag and let it rest in the fridge for half an hour.

Preheat the oven to 160°C. Butter the recesses of a 12-hole tart tin.

Dust a work surface and a rolling pin with potato flour. Divide the dough into 2 equal portions. Roll out 1 portion of the dough thinly and use a round 8cm pastry cutter to stamp out 10–12 rounds. Using a palette knife under each round for support, lift the rounds into the recesses of the prepared tin and press them in gently. Fill each case with 20g mincemeat (slightly over 1 tablespoon).

Roll out the second portion of dough and, this time, stamp out rounds with a round 7cm pastry cutter. Again, with the support of a palette knife, lift them into position on top of the mincemeat to make lids and press down the edges. Brush the tops lightly with the beaten egg and make little 2 cuts in the top of each pastry lid with a knife to allow air to escape during cooking. Bake until the mince pies are golden, about 15 minutes.

Cool the mince pies on a wire rack. When they are cold, pack them in an airtight box with baking parchment between each layer.

indian yogurt dessert

Typically Indian meals conclude with wonderful fresh fruit, perfectly ripened. Many Indian sweets are full of sugar and are served on special occasions to welcome guests when they arrive. *Shrikhand*, although traditionally served with vegetable curries, also makes a delicious dessert. I love the creamy yogurt mixed with saffron, the beautiful perfume of the rosewater and the crunch of the pine nuts. Kumquats complement this dish beautifully.

SERVES 4

Generous pinch of saffron
2 tablespoons boiling water
500ml Greek sheep's yogurt
½ teaspoon cardamom seeds, crushed
2 tablespoons rosewater
2 tablespoons maple syrup
2 tablespoons pine nuts or chopped cashews
2 tablespoons raisins

Dissolve the saffron in the boiling water. Mix with all the ingredients. Serve chilled.

moroccan crème brûlée

François Massialot (1660–1733) is credited as the first chef to have written a recipe for crème brûlée, in his *Le Cuisinier Roïal et Bourgeois* (Paris 1691). A notable client of his was Philippe II of Orléans, who became Regent in 1715. The Regent, a passionate viol player, chose the leading virtuoso, Antoine Forqueray (1672–1745) to teach him. Forqueray was clearly a favourite – the Regent reimbursed him the potentially ruinous loss of 100,000 *livres* that he incurred investing in the Mississippi Company. Might not Forqueray have eaten Massialot's crème brûlée at the Palais Royal?

This recipe is inspired by the crème brûlée I ate in Le Sirocco, a charming Moroccan restaurant in the rue des Gobelins, Paris 13ᵉ. The chef kindly told me his ingredients. Interestingly, Massailot's original also uses orange flower water and zest, in his case, lime.

SERVES 6

Butter, for greasing
540ml cream
30ml milk
1 teaspoon cardamom seeds, crushed
Grated zest of 1 lemon
3 tablespoons orange flower water
2 heaped tablespoons fragrant honey
6 egg yolks
2 tablespoons blanched almonds, ground in a food processor
1 teaspoon ground cinnamon
1 teaspoon coriander seeds, crushed using a pestle and mortar

Preheat the oven to 150C. Butter 6 ramekins.

Put the the cream, milk, cardamom seeds and lemon zest in a saucepan set over a low heat and heat until almost boiling. Alternatively, put them in a bowl and heat in a microwave oven on a low setting until almost boiling, about 3 minutes. Add 2 tablespoons of the orange flower water. Using an electric whisk, beat together the honey and egg yolks until pale and fluffy. Reduce the speed setting to low and beat in the hot cream mixture.

Divide the custard between the ramekins. Place in a bain-marie with enough boiling water to reach halfway up the sides of the dishes. Bake until golden and set, about 30 minutes. Leave to cool, then refrigerate.

Soak the almonds in 1 tablespoon orange flower water for 10 minutes. Mix in the cinnamon and crushed coriander seeds. Shortly before serving, preheat the grill on a medium setting. Sprinkle the mixture on the top of each ramekin and, with care, lightly brown the nuts under the grill.

paskha

This rich, uncooked Russian cheesecake is made at Easter (*Paskha*) to celebrate the end of Lent. It is traditionally made in a pyramid mould, symbolising the Church, and marked with the orthodox cross. The Paskha cake is blessed in church before being eaten. It certainly breaks the Lenten fast in an unabashed and flamboyant fashion.

SERVES 8–10

90g butter, softened
600g cream cheese
175g Greek yogurt
1 egg yolk
2 tablespoons maple syrup or fragrant honey
90g dried pineapple, finely chopped
90g dried apricots, finely chopped
90g sultanas
45g blanched almonds, chopped
45g Brazil nuts, chopped
60g toasted flaked almonds

Combine the butter, cream cheese and yogurt in a food processor.

In a large bowl, whisk the egg yolk and maple syrup together until pale and fluffy. Beat in the cheese mixture. Add the dried fruit and chopped nuts and mix everything together.

Line an 18cm sieve with some cheesecloth or a handkerchief, leaving 10cm of cloth overhanging the edge. Sit the lined sieve over a small mixing bowl and spoon the paskha mixture inside it. Tie the ends of the cloth firmly together around the paskha mixture. Place a saucer of a lesser diameter than the sieve on top of the paskha mixture in the sieve. Press the saucer down with weights. Transfer to the fridge and leave there to drain and chill for 24 hours.

Carefully dry-roast the flaked almonds in a frying pan until they become a light golden colour. Leave to cool.

Turn out the paskha onto a serving plate. Press the flaked almonds all over the surface.

Transfer the paskha to the fridge and leave it there until 30 minutes before you intend to serve it, then bring it out and leave it come to room temperature.

ice creams and sorbets

Can you imagine life without a fridge? In parts of Asia, as early as the third century BC, people would store blocks of ice or snow in a dry underground place to cool food. Here lie the remote origins of the ice cream and water ice or sorbet. Sei Shonagon, in eleventh-century Japan, delighted in 'chips of ice mixed with fruit juice and served in a silver bowl'. Middle Eastern sherbets, in which we find the roots of the Italian *sorbetto* and the French *sorbet*, were originally made of fruit juice and honey. And there is a description from the sixteenth-century of Indian *kulfi* in the royal kitchens of the Emperor Akbar (1542–1605), made with reduced milk, saffron and pistachios. (See Elizabeth David's fascinating social study of ice and ices: *Harvest of Cold Months*.)

European ice creams and sorbets probably appeared in early seventeenth-century Italy, and were then taken up by the court of Louis XIV and in Spain, then made their way to other European courts. The writings of early cookery writer Lady Anne Fanshawe (1625–80) reveal that she saw iced confections at the court of Philip IV of Spain (see Ivan Day's blog: *Food History Jottings*, 5 April 2012). She described how the 'King and Queen eat together twice a week in public, with their children' and that their meal included 'drinking water... cold with snow'. Anne gave a very early recipe for 'Icy Cream' in her manuscript *Book of Cookery and Medical Receipts* in the mid 1660s:

Take three pints of the best cream, boyle it with a blade of Mace, or else perfume it with orange flower water or ambergris. Sweeten the cream with sugar, let it stand till it is quite cold. Then put it into Boxes, either of silver or of tin. Then take ice chopped into small pieces and put it into a tub and so the Boxes in the Ice covering them all over. And let them stand in the ice two hours, and the Cream will come to be Ice in the Boxes. Then turn them out on to a salvar with some of the Seasoned Cream. So serve it up to the Table.

Anne accidentally misses out the vital salt or saltpetre necessary to reduce the temperature. The highly prized ambergris comes from the sperm whale; happily, orange flower water was far more common.

In the first year of his Restoration, Charles II built an icehouse in St James' Park, perhaps inspired by his Parisian sojourn and encouraged by his friends, the Fanshawes. The poet Edmund Waller celebrated Charles' improvements:

Yonder the harvest of cold months laid up,
Gives a fresh coolness to the Royal Cup;
There Ice like Christal, firm and never lost,
Tempers hot July with December's frost
Winter's dark prison; where he cannot flie,
Though the warm Spring, his enemy, grows nigh.
Strange! that extremes should thus preserve the Snow
High on the Alpes, and in deep Caves below!

vanilla ice cream

Despite its name, I like my ice cream made from a custard that is half cream, half milk, with 5 egg yolks to 600ml cream and milk. It can be made either on the stove or in a microwave oven on a low setting. I use the latter. If you are using the microwave, should the custard start to curdle, quickly blitz it with a hand-held blender to rescue the situation; the final result will be marginally grainier than an ice cream made with a perfect custard, but those eating it will probably not notice.

Using an ice cream maker produces a creamy ice cream and makes the whole process easier. I have an inexpensive machine. Its stainless steel bowl should be put in the freezer for 10 hours before making ice cream. Mine lives in the freezer, ready for impromptu ice cream making. If your timing is perfect you can eat the ice cream straight from the machine.

If the ice cream is fully frozen you should put it in the fridge for about 20 minutes before you are ready to serve, so that it can thaw slightly. Should the ice cream be still a bit soft, leave it in the freezer.

SERVES 6

300ml cream
300ml milk
5 egg yolks
135g fragrant honey
2 teaspoons good-quality vanilla essence

Put the cream and milk in a saucepan set over a high heat and bring almost to boiling point. With an electric beater, whisk together the egg yolks, honey and vanilla until the mixture is pale and fluffy. Set the beater to a low speed and pour on the hot cream mixture.

To make a custard in a microwave oven, put the mixture in a bowl and cook on a low setting, stirring regularly, until it thickens, 2–3 minutes. To make the custard on the hob, stir the egg-and-cream mixture constantly over a low heat until it begins to set and thinly coats the back of the spoon, about 8 minutes. Whichever method you choose, ensure the custard does not boil or it will curdle. Leave to cool, then refrigerate for at least 1 hour.

Churn the custard in an ice cream maker until thick, about 20 minutes. Transfer to a plastic box and freeze.

VARIATION

– For raspberry or blackcurrant ripple, add 100g blackcurrant or raspberry purée to the ice cream maker for the last few seconds of churning.

ginger ice cream

Ginger ice cream is an excellent accompaniment to a rich chocolate cake. I make chocolate cake in the same manner as the Catalan Chestnut Chocolate Cake (see page 240), but omitting the chestnuts and only using the 100ml of cream that goes into the cake itself. Once it has cooled, I dust it with 1 tablespoon best-quality cocoa.

SERVES 6

300ml cream
300ml milk
5 egg yolks
135g maple syrup
90g Honeyed Stem Ginger (see page 266), chopped
1 tablespoon ground ginger

Put the cream and milk in a saucepan set over a high heat and bring almost to boiling point.

With an electric beater, whisk together the egg yolks, maple syrup, stem ginger and ground ginger until the mixture is pale and fluffy. Set the beater to a low speed and pour on the hot cream mixture.

To make a custard in a microwave oven, put the mixture in a bowl and cook on a low setting, stirring regularly, until it thickens, 2–3 minutes. To make the custard on the hob, stir the egg-and-cream mixture constantly over a low heat until it begins to set and thinly coats the back of the spoon, about 8 minutes. Whichever method you choose, ensure the custard does not boil or it will curdle. Leave to cool, then refrigerate for at least 1 hour.

Churn the custard in an ice cream maker until thick, about 20 minutes. Transfer to a plastic box and freeze.

About 20 minutes before serving, transfer the ice cream to the fridge to soften. (Alternatively, soften it in a microwave oven on a high setting for about 10 seconds.)

persian bastani ice cream

This recipe is inspired by the amazing Iranian saffron that our harpsichord student Aydin brought us from his mother in Iran. The quality of its taste was a revelation. The saffron fields lie in North-Eastern Iran and their flowers are picked in the autumn. There are only three stigmas in each flower; 210,000 stigmas (70,000 flowers) make half a kilo of saffron.

I have chosen to use an European egg custard in this recipe. For me, the exotic marriage of saffron, rosewater and pistachios is irresistible.

SERVES 6

300ml cream
300ml milk
Generous pinch of saffron
135g fragrant honey
5 egg yolks
3 tablespoons rosewater
60g pistachio nuts, chopped

Put the cream, milk and saffron in a saucepan set over a high heat and bring almost to boiling point. Give the saffron cream a stir and leave for half an hour to infuse.

With an electric beater, whisk the honey and egg yolks together until they go pale and fluffy. Reheat the saffron cream to simmering point and pour it over the egg mixture, whisking gently all the time.

To make a custard in a microwave oven, put the mixture in a bowl and cook on a low setting, stirring regularly, until it thickens, 2–3 minutes. To make the custard on the hob, stir the egg-and-cream mixture constantly over a low heat until it begins to set and thinly coats the back of the spoon, about 8 minutes. Whichever method you choose, ensure the custard does not boil or it will curdle. Leave to cool. Stir in the rosewater and pistachios, then refrigerate for at least 1 hour.

Churn the custard in an ice cream maker until thick, about 20 minutes. Transfer to a plastic box and freeze.

About 20 minutes before serving, transfer the ice cream to the fridge to soften. (Alternatively, soften it in a microwave oven on a high setting for about 10 seconds.)

cardamom ice cream
with coconut milk

This ice cream is inspired by Indian *kulfi*. But like with the Persian *Bastani* Ice Cream (see page 223), I have chosen to use an European egg custard. The coconut milk gives a beautiful light texture. Serve with Macaroons (see page 251).

SERVES 6

300ml cream
300ml coconut milk
Grated zest of 1 lime
½ teaspoon cardamom seeds, crushed
5 egg yolks
135g fragrant honey

Put the cream, milk, lime zest and cardamom seeds in a saucepan set over a high heat and bring almost to boiling point.

With an electric beater, whisk together the egg yolks and honey until the mixture is pale and fluffy. Set the beater to a low speed and pour on the hot, spiced cream mixture.

To make a custard in a microwave oven, put the mixture in a bowl and cook on a low setting, stirring regularly, until it thickens, 2–3 minutes. To make the custard on the hob, stir the egg-and-cream mixture constantly over a low heat until it begins to set and thinly coats the back of the spoon, about 8 minutes. Whichever method you choose, ensure the custard does not boil or it will curdle. Leave to cool, then refrigerate for at least 1 hour.

Churn the custard in an ice cream maker until thick, about 20 minutes. Transfer to a plastic box and freeze.

About 20 minutes before serving, transfer the ice cream to the fridge to soften. (Alternatively, soften it in a microwave oven on a high setting for about 10 seconds.)

seville orange ice cream

Nowadays, most of the Seville oranges that are grown in Spain are exported to Britain for marmalade. But the bitter orange tree is found throughout the Orient and is grown for its flowers, to make orange flower water and the beautifully scented essential oil, Neroli; its oranges are used for liqueurs, such as Cointreau. Seville orange juice can be used in place of lemon juice in vinaigrettes; it also makes a fabulous ice cream.

SERVES 8

4 Seville oranges
400ml cream
200ml milk
160g mild honey
6 egg yolks
Grated zest of 2 Seville oranges
1½ teaspoons good-quality vanilla essence
200ml Seville orange juice, chilled

Use the Seville oranges to make receptacles for your ice cream. Cut them in half, squeeze out the juice (to go towards the 200ml you need to make this recipe), scoop out and discard the pulp and tidy up the skins, then freeze them.

Put the cream and milk in a saucepan set over a high heat and bring almost to boiling point.

With an electric beater, whisk together the honey, egg yolks, orange zest and vanilla until the mixture is pale and fluffy. Set the beater to a low speed and pour on the hot cream mixture.

To make a custard in a microwave oven, put the mixture in a bowl and cook on a low setting, stirring regularly, until it thickens, 2–3 minutes. To make the custard on the hob, stir the egg-and-cream mixture constantly over a low heat until it begins to set and thinly coats the back of the spoon, about 8 minutes. Whichever method you choose, ensure the custard does not boil or it will curdle. Leave to cool, then stir in the orange juice. Refrigerate for at least 1 hour.

Churn the custard in an ice cream maker until thick, about 20 minutes. Fill the orange skins generously with the ice cream and freeze.

About 20 minutes before serving, transfer the ice cream to the fridge to soften. (Alternatively, soften it in a microwave oven on a high setting for about 10 seconds.)

frozen raspberry sorbet

Stunning to look at, frozen raspberry sorbet is an incredible ruby red and wonderfully quick to make. One time, I made it for the Christmas Bombe (see page 230) using my sister's frozen loganberries and the colour was even more vibrant. Delicious paired with Vanilla Ice Cream (see page 221) and decorated with toasted flaked almonds, raspberries and a sprig of mint or lemon verbena.

SERVES 6

500g frozen raspberries
Juice of 1 orange
Juice of 1 lemon
125g maple syrup or mild honey

Pulverise the frozen raspberries with the orange and lemon juice and maple syrup in a food processor. If the sorbet pulp seems too strong, add a little water, about 45ml.

Churn the raspberry pulp in an ice cream maker until thick. This will not take long because the raspberries are still very cold, about 8 minutes. Transfer to a plastic box and freeze.

About 15 minutes before serving, transfer the sorbet to the fridge to soften. (Alternatively, soften it in a microwave oven on a high setting for about 8 seconds.)

VARIATION

Add 4 tablespoons Cointreau to the raspberry purée
in the food processor.

lemon sorbet

Fresh and tangy, lemon sorbet is the perfect refreshing treat on a hot summer's day in the garden.

SERVES 6

300g mild honey
300ml water
300ml lemon juice
Grated zest of 2 lemons

Gently heat the honey and water in a saucepan and simmer for about 3 minutes. Leave the syrup to cool, then stir in the lemon juice and zest. Chill the mixture in the fridge for 1 hour.

Churn the syrup in an ice cream maker until thick, about 15 minutes. Transfer to a plastic box and freeze.

About 15 minutes before serving, transfer the sorbet to the fridge to soften. (Alternatively, soften it in a microwave oven on a high setting for about 8 seconds.)

blackcurrant sorbet

Blackcurrant sorbet, made with fruit from the garden, is for me the ultimate sorbet flavour. It marries exquisitely with Vanilla Ice Cream (see page 221) or Lemon Sorbet (see opposite page).

SERVES 6

125g mild honey
125ml water
500g blackcurrants
Juice of 1 lemon

Gently heat the honey and water in a saucepan and simmer for about 3 minutes. Add the blackcurrants and simmer for a further 3 minutes.

Blend the blackcurrant syrup in a food processor and strain. Leave to cool, then stir in the lemon juice.

Churn the syrup in an ice cream maker until thick, about 15 minutes. Transfer to a plastic box and freeze.

About 15 minutes before serving, transfer the sorbet to the fridge to soften. (Alternatively, soften it in a microwave oven on a high setting for about 8 seconds.)

VARIATION

Add 4 tablespoons *crème de cassis* with the lemon juice.

christmas bombe

With a bright, beautiful raspberry layer on the outside, this bombe makes a bold impact – a spectacular finale to Christmas dinner. Its shape is appropriately reminiscent of the Christmas pudding that the family has quietly rejected – you can even stick a sprig of holly on top if you are so moved. It has intense flavours to delight and it is light after the Christmas Day Mock Goose (see page 123).

Freeze the mould before you begin making the bombe, as it helps to stick the first layer, the raspberry sorbet, to it.

SERVES 12

1 quantity Frozen Raspberry Sorbet (see page 226)
1½ quantities Persian Bastani Ice Cream (see page 223)

Freeze a 1.5 litre bombe mould.

Spoon the raspberry sorbet straight from the ice cream maker into the chilled mould, pressing it up against the walls of the mould in a layer that is 3–4 cm thick. Use a spatula to spread the sorbet evenly right up to the top edge of the mould. Ensure there is plenty of space left in the centre to receive the ice cream later. Cover the mould with its lid and freeze for 1 hour.

If any of the sorbet has sunk down into the mould after the initial freezing period, use a spatula to encourage it back up to the top again. Fill the middle of the mould with the Persian Bastani ice cream, once again, straight from the ice cream maker. Replace the lid of the mould and freeze for 12 hours.

About 15–20 minutes before you wish to serve the bombe, transfer the mould from the freezer to the fridge.

To serve, run the hot water tap and put the mould under it for a moment or two. Dry the outside of the mould and run a knife around the edge of the bombe to assist in releasing the sorbet. Invert the bombe onto a serving dish, remove the mould and serve immediately.

CAKES, BISCUITS AND TREATS

swiss carrot cake

Delicious Swiss *Rüeblitorte* is believed to be the oldest form of carrot cake, with recipes dating back to the nineteenth century. Carrot cake became popular in Britain during the Second World War, when sugar was rationed and the government strongly promoted carrots in the Dig for Victory campaign as an alternative to sugar. This Swiss carrot cake, made with nuts, is wonderfully light and the combination of roasted hazelnuts, moist carrots and lemon zest is extremely tasty.

SERVES 8

Butter, for greasing
125g hazelnuts
3 eggs, separated
125g honey
150g carrots, grated
50g ground almonds
Grated zest and juice of 1 lemon
½ teaspoon bicarbonate of soda

ICING (OPTIONAL)

150g cream cheese
50g butter
50g honey
1 teaspoon vanilla essence

Preheat the oven to 170°C. Line the base of a 19cm springform cake tin with baking parchment, and butter the tin and paper.

Roast the hazelnuts in the oven, about 8 minutes. Put the roasted nuts into a food processor and, using the pulse button, chop them roughly.

Beat the egg yolks and honey until thick and creamy. Stir in the carrots, hazelnuts, ground almonds, and the lemon zest and juice. In another bowl, sieve the bicarbonate of soda into the egg whites and whisk until thick. Fold in the nut mixture and spoon into the prepared tin.

Bake until the cake is golden and the sides of the cake come away from the tin, about 25 minutes. Leave to cool in the tin, then position the cake on a serving plate.

To make the icing, mix all the ingredients in the food processor. Spread on the cooled cake.

VARIATION

Substitute almonds for half the hazelnuts.

kibrizli cake

One evening, after a concert we had given, my aunt surprised
us with this unusual syrupy cake flavoured with lemon, honey and
sesame seeds. It is a Middle Eastern cake that is popular in Egypt,
Syria and Jordan.

SERVES 8–10

CAKE

Butter, for greasing
6 eggs, separated
250g honey
Grated zest of 2 large lemons
250g ground almonds
½ teaspoon bicarbonate of soda, sieved
150ml water
2 teaspoons sesame seeds

SYRUP

75ml water
100g honey
Juice of 2 large lemons

Preheat the oven to 160°C. Line the base of a deep 23cm springform
cake tin with baking parchment, and butter the tin and paper.

Whisk the egg yolks and the honey until creamy and pale. Add the
lemon zest, almonds, bicarbonate of soda and water and whisk until
smooth. In a separate bowl, use a clean whisk to whisk the egg whites
until stiff, then gently fold in the yolk-and-almond mixture. Pour into
the prepared cake tin and sprinkle with the sesame seeds.

Bake until the cake is firm and comes away from the sides of the tin,
about 30 minutes.

Meanwhile, make the syrup. Boil the water and honey in a saucepan
until the mixture is syrupy. Remove from the heat and stir in the
lemon juice. Leave to cool.

When the cake is cooked, spoon the cool syrup gradually and evenly
over the hot cake. Leave the cake to cool in the tin. Then loosen the
sides carefully with a knife and turn out.

sephardic orange cake

My family and friends think of this wonderful cake as my signature tune. But the truth is that the idea came from Claudia Roden's *A Book of Middle Eastern Food*, which I gave to my aunt for Christmas after my first term at York University. I have been making it ever since and, I have to say, I like my version using honey. It was my mother's idea to put best-quality chocolate on top at our wedding. The cake keeps well and can be made several days in advance, kept in a plastic box or bag. It is good served with cream.

The use of ground almonds is specially for the Jewish Passover, when grains are forbidden if they have had contact with moisture for more than 18 minutes.

SERVES 12–16

4 oranges
2 tablespoons water
6 eggs
225g ground almonds
225g honey
1 teaspoon bicarbonate of soda
170g dark chocolate (70 per cent cocoa solids)
20g butter, plus extra for greasing

Preheat the oven to 170°C. Line the base of a 26cm springform cake tin with baking parchment, and butter the tin and paper. (You can use a 22cm tin diameter for a deeper cake.)

Quarter the oranges (unpeeled, pips and all), place them in a covered dish with the water and cook in a microwave oven on a high setting until tender, about 15 minutes. Alternatively, boil them in a covered pan in about 100ml water until soft, between 1½–2 hours, watching that there is enough water. Then blend in a food processor. Add the eggs, almonds and honey and blend again. Sieve in the bicarbonate of soda and blend once more. Pour the mixture into the prepared tin. Bake until the cake is golden brown and comes away from the sides of the tin, about 40 minutes. Prod the cake with a skewer – if some of the cake sticks to the skewer when it is withdrawn, cook it a little longer. But this cake should be moist. Leave to cool in the tin. Place on a serving plate.

Melt the chocolate and butter in the microwave on a low setting or in a bowl set over a saucepan of gently simmering water. Stir to combine. Spread the mixture over the cake and leave it to cool.

bûche de noël

In France the original *Bûche de Noël* (Christmas log) was a large log traditionally from a fruit tree, such as an olive or cherry, which was brought inside on Christmas Eve. After being carried around the table three times by the oldest and youngest members of the family, it was put on the hearth and burnt. As it combusted they blessed it by throwing hot wine on it, to ensure a good grape harvest. This large log was later substituted by a smaller branch, which was set in the middle of the table and decorated with sweet meats – treats for the family and guests. In 1879, this branch was magically transformed into a cake by the Parisian *pâtissier*, Antoine Charadot.

SERVES 10

6 large eggs, separated
150g honey
250g dark chocolate (70 per cent cocoa solids), split into pieces
30g butter, plus extra for greasing
300ml cream
300g raspberries

Preheat the oven to 170°C. Lightly butter a 28 × 38cm Swiss roll tin and line with baking parchment.

Whisk the egg yolks and honey until pale. Melt the chocolate with the butter in a bowl set over a saucepan of gently simmering water, or put the chocolate and butter in a bowl and melt in a microwave oven on a low setting for about 2–3 minutes. Stir well. Stir in the egg mixture.

In another bowl, beat the egg whites until stiff. With a large metal spoon, carefully fold the beaten whites into the chocolate. Spoon the cake mixture into the prepared tin and bake for about 12 minutes until risen and firm to the touch. Check that the mixture has set by inserting a skewer into the cake – if it does not come out clean, bake for an extra 5 minutes or until set. Leave to cool in the tin.

Whip the cream and set aside. Follow the instructions given on page 135 to remove the cake from the tin, then spread the cream on the cake and scatter the raspberries on top, leaving a gap and rolling up the cake as directed on pages 134–5. Any filling that is pushed along the cake as you roll will end up on the gap you left uncovered at the far end of the cake, but if any of the filling spills over the edge, gently tuck it back in. Carefully transfer the log to a large plate. Do not worry if any cracks appear – they enhance the log-like appearance.

chocolate and almond cake

When I went to live in Toledo for five months I allowed myself two cookery books, Elizabeth David's *French Provincial Cooking* was one. I adapted her recipe for *Gâteau au chocolat et aux amandes* and it worked so well, I still make it regularly. I love its simplicity – the crumb is beautifully moist and light. It is excellent as a dessert with some fruit for an impromptu meal or for tea time, served with whipped cream.

SERVES 8

3 eggs, separated
85g mild honey
115g dark chocolate (70 per cent cocoa solids)
85g butter, plus extra for greasing
85g ground almonds
1 tablespoon cocoa powder

Preheat the oven to 145°C. Line the base of a shallow 20cm cake tin with baking parchment and lightly butter the inside of the tin, including the paper.

Whisk the egg yolks and honey until the mixture becomes pale. Melt the chocolate with the butter in a bowl set over a saucepan of gently simmering water, or put the chocolate and butter in a bowl and melt in a microwave oven on a low setting for about 2–3 minutes. Stir well. When the chocolate and butter have melted, add them with the ground almonds to the honey-and-egg mixture and stir. Using an electric whisk, beat the egg whites until stiff. Fold in the chocolate mixture.

Pour the cake mixture into the prepared cake tin. Bake until firm, about 25–30 minutes. Leave the cake in the tin to cool completely, then turn it out onto a serving plate.

Dust the cooled cake with cocoa powder to serve.

catalan chestnut chocolate cake

Chestnut trees grow throughout Catalonia and chestnuts were part of the staple diet of peasants, who would dry them and make them into bread. But chocolate was a novelty, introduced from Mexico in the sixteenth century, notionally by the Spanish conquistador Cortés. The Catalan bourgeoisie would probably have procured their solid-block chocolate from Bayonne in the French Basque country, where it was first made by Jewish émigrés expelled by the Spanish Inquisition.

This cake is essentially a rich chocolate mousse, so serve it in small slices. In the photograph opposite I have decorated it with Moroccan Oranges (see page 212) as well as toasted blanched almonds.

SERVES 10–12

400g plain chocolate
100g unsalted butter
6 eggs, separated
100g honey
140g vacuum-packed chestnuts, chopped
300ml cream
Toasted blanched almonds, to decorate

Preheat the oven to 170°C. Line the base of a 26cm springform cake tin with baking parchment and butter the tin and paper.

Melt the chocolate with the butter in a bowl set over a saucepan of gently simmering water, or put the chocolate and butter in a bowl and melt in a microwave oven on a low setting for about 2–3 minutes. Stir well.

Whisk the egg yolks and honey until pale, then stir the mixture into the chocolate. Add the chestnuts and 100ml of the cream. With an electric beater, whisk the egg whites until stiff. Fold in the chocolate mixture. Pour the batter into the prepared tin and bake for about 25 minutes until gently springy to the touch. Leave to cool in the tin.

Run a knife round the edge of the cake to loosen it. Place it on a serving plate. Whip the remaining 200ml cream, spread the whipped cream over the cake and decorate with toasted blanched almonds.

VARIATION

For a deliciously rich chocolate mousse for 6, follow the method for making the cake mixture, using half the quantities of chocolate, butter, eggs, honey and cream and omitting the chestnuts. (Add 1 tablespoon either Cointreau or Cognac to the mousse mixture, if desired.) Divide the mixture into 6 ramekins and refrigerate for 1 hour before serving.

sicilian ricotta cake

When the Mediterranean was perceived as the centre of the world, Sicily became a highly attractive prize and, as a consequence, was colonised by the Greeks, Romans and Arabs, and then ruled by Spain, Austria and Constantinople. The Greeks brought ricotta and honey to Sicily, as well as wine and olives, and the Arabs arrived with exotic new fruits and vegetables and sophisticated new growing techniques. The result is a cuisine of kaleidoscopic influences, full of delights such as orange blossoms, raisins, pine nuts, almonds, pistachios, chocolate, saffron, capers, Marsala, orange and lemon zest, and jasmine.

Sicilians favour ewes'-milk ricotta to make their finest desserts. Here, I have substituted colourful cranberries dried in apple concentrate for the more typical candied peel.

SERVES 8

Butter, for greasing
500g ricotta
150g honey
5 eggs, separated
2 teaspoons orange flower water
1 tablespoon grated lemon zest
75g dried cranberries

Preheat the oven to 170°C. Line the base of a 22cm springform cake tin with baking parchment and butter the tin and paper.

Mix the ricotta, honey, egg yolks, orange flower water and lemon zest in a food processor. Beat the egg whites until stiff and fold them into the ricotta mixture. Fold in the cranberries and spoon the mixture carefully into the prepared cake tin.

Bake until the cheese cake is golden brown, about 30 minutes. Leave the cake to cool in the tin, then transfer to a serving plate.

lemon cheesecake

Decorate this cheesecake with passion fruit, or pomegranate seeds with toasted pistachios, or chopped and toasted blanched almonds.

SERVES 8–10

75g ground almonds
75g potato flour
75g butter, plus extra for greasing
215g honey
4 eggs, separated
600g best-quality cream cheese
1½ teaspoons vanilla extract
Grated zest and juice of 1 large lemon

TOPPING

160ml soured cream
1 tablespoon honey
2 teaspoons lemon juice

Preheat the oven to 150°C. Line the base of a 22cm springform cake tin with baking parchment and butter the tin and paper.

To make the cheesecake base, blend the almonds, potato flour, butter and 75g of the honey in a food processor. Press the mixture into the base of the prepared cake tin. Bake until light brown, about 10 minutes.

Using an electric beater, whisk the egg yolks and remaining honey until creamy and pale. Beat in the cream cheese, vanilla, lemon zest and juice. Whisk the egg whites until stiff and fold into the cheese mixture. Pour the mixture over the cheesecake base. Bake until the top sets and becomes light golden, about 30 minutes.

To prepare the topping, mix the soured cream, honey and lemon juice. Spoon the mixture over the top of the cooked cheesecake. Return the cake to the oven until the topping has become glossy and acquired a golden tinge, about 8 minutes, then leave to cool.

To remove the cheesecake from the tin, work around the edge carefully with a sharp knife and undo the spring of the cake tin. Using a fish slice, or possibly two, ease the cake onto a flat serving plate. If it seems too precarious to do so, leave it on the base on a pretty plate.

Chill in the fridge for at least 1 hour. Then decorate the top further if you wish, but put the cheesecake back in the fridge afterwards, where it will keep for several days. About 20 minutes before serving, bring the cake to room temperature.

florentines

Crisp and buttery, florentines are a gorgeous treat.

MAKES ABOUT 20

60g butter, plus extra for greasing
120g honey
60g potato flour
60g blanched almonds, lightly crushed
60g flaked almonds
60g sunflower seeds
60g dried pineapple
60g dried cranberries
60g sultanas
2 tablespoons orange zest
150g dark chocolate (70 per cent cocoa solids), split into pieces

Preheat the oven to 150°C. Line 2 baking sheets that each measure 28cm × 38cm with buttered baking paper.

In a large saucepan, melt the butter and honey. Bring briefly to the boil, then remove the pan from the heat. Stir in the potato flour and add all the other ingredients, save the chocolate.

Drop level tablespoons of the mixture onto the prepared trays, spacing them about 3cm apart. Flatten the mounds with the back of spoon.

Bake until dry and set, 10–15 minutes. Remove the trays from the oven and wait for the Florentines to cool and harden, about 10 minutes. Then carefully place the delicate biscuits on a wire rack with the flat sides facing upwards.

Melt the chocolate in a bowl set over a saucepan of gently simmering water, or in a microwave oven on a low setting for about 3 minutes.

Using a metal spatula, spread the melted chocolate over the smooth side of each Florentine. When the chocolate has nearly set, mark swirling lines in it with a fork. Leave on a wire rack with the chocolate-coated sides facing upwards until completely cool.

Pack the cooled Florentines in an airtight box with greaseproof paper between each layer.

chocolate brownies

These delicious, intensely chocolatey brownies are superb for taking with you on a walk. If you are eating them at home, serve the brownies with a dollop of cream or Vanilla Ice Cream (see page 221).

When cooking chocolate, whether as brownies or as a cake, be extremely careful not to scorch it or your treat will become bitter. If the chocolate looks in danger of darkening too much during cooking, place a sheet of baking parchment over the baking tin.

MAKES 15

175g mixture of almonds, cashews and walnuts
200g dark chocolate (70 per cent cocoa solids), split into pieces
150g butter
60g ground almonds
4 eggs, lightly beaten
200g honey
½ teaspoon bicarbonate of soda
1 teaspoon cream of tartar

Preheat the oven to 170°C. Line a 20cm × 30cm baking tin with some baking parchment.

In a food processor, using the pulse button, chop the nuts roughly. Place them on a baking sheet and roast them in the oven for 8 minutes.

Melt the chocolate with the butter in a bowl set over a saucepan of gently simmering water, or put the chocolate and butter in a bowl and melt in a microwave oven on a low setting for about 2–3 minutes. Stir well. Add the roasted nuts, ground almonds, eggs and honey. Sieve in the bicarbonate of soda and cream of tartar.

Pour the mixture into the prepared baking tin and bake until the top is springy to the touch and a skewer inserted into the centre of the cake comes out a bit gooey, about 25 minutes. Leave the cake to cool in the tin until completely cold. Then remove it from the tin and cut it into 15 brownies.

chocolate truffles

Using top-quality dark chocolate of 70 per cent cocoa solids is the secret for excellent chocolate truffles.

MAKES ABOUT 25 TRUFFLES

150g dark chocolate (70 per cent cocoa solids), split into pieces
150g cream
30g unsalted butter
2 tablespoons Cointreau or Cognac
About 4 tablespoons good-quality pure cocoa powder

Pulverize the chocolate in a food processor.

Heat the cream and butter in a saucepan over a medium heat until almost boiling. Switch on the food processor and pour the hot cream through the funnel onto the ground chocolate until the combined mixture is smooth. Add the Cointreau or Cognac and blend.

Put the chocolate mixture into a bowl and leave it to cool. Then cover it with clingfilm and refrigerate for about 2 hours until thick.

If you intend to present the truffles in small paper cases, separate and arrange the cases, ready to receive the truffles. Sift the cocoa powder onto a plate. Roll 1 teaspoon of the chocolate mixture into a ball and roll the ball in the cocoa powder. Place it in a paper case or on a plate. Avoid handling the mixture more than necessary because it will melt! Repeat with the remaining chocolate mixture. The truffles will keep in the fridge for several days in a sealed plastic box, or in the freezer for a month.

VARIATIONS

– Add the grated zest of ½ orange to the simmering cream.
– Add 120g toasted flaked almonds or 100g Honeyed Stem Ginger (see page 266) to the chocolate mixture once it has hardened in the fridge.
– Instead of rolling the truffles in cocoa powder, they can be coated in a layer of pure chocolate. First, spread out some baking parchment. Melt 200g chocolate with 4 tablespoons cream, either in a bowl set over a saucepan of simmering water, or in a microwave oven on a low setting. Remove from the heat. Using a little cocoa powder to stop the mixture sticking to your hands, roll 1 teaspoon of the chocolate mixture into a ball. With 2 cocktail sticks, one firmly pushed into the middle of the truffle and the other to help manoeuvre it, dip the truffle in the melted chocolate, give it a thin coating, then quickly place it on the baking parchment. Refrigerate to set. When the chocolate coating has set hard, place the truffles in paper cases or on a plate.

afternoon tea

Concerts on a Sunday afternoon, followed by a delicious tea, are received with great enthusiasm – the tea quite as much as the concert! Ease the stress and make all the cakes and biscuits the day before, not least if you are performing in the concert yourself. If you can find a fragrant Charentais melon, it needs to be cut into cubes as close as possible to serving time. And don't forget to put the tea urn on before the concert begins! Spread a large table with a pretty tablecloth and decorate with a vase of flowers, from the garden, if possible. When the Camellia is in flower, I scatter the blooms over the table or around the rim of the cake plates. Fresh lemon verbena tea is wonderfully thirst quenching and very popular. I nurse my trusty verbena plant through the winter by wrapping it up in fleece.

SERVES 35–40

Sephardic Orange Cake *page 237*

Sicilian Ricotta Cake *page 242*

Chocolate Brownies *page 246*

Macaroons *page 251*

Persian Biscuits *page 253*

Squares of Charentais melon with cocktail sticks.

TO DRINK

Infusions: fresh lemon verbena and mint from the garden

Earl Grey tea, artisan apple juice

macaroons

Macaroons were popular as light refreshments in the eighteenth and nineteenth centuries and were served with wine. They are also a speciality for Passover with the Sephardic Jewish community. Recipes for macaroons appear all around the Mediterranean, with delightful local variations.

These macaroons would happily accompany a mint tea or, if you drink it, a cup of coffee. They are also excellent with ice cream or a fruit salad.

MAKES ABOUT 14

200g ground almonds
120g honey
Grated zest of 1 orange
½ teaspoon cardamom seeds, crushed
1 small egg white
90g flaked almonds or 120g pine nuts, to coat

Preheat the oven to 150°C. Line a 28cm × 38cm baking tray with baking parchment.

Blend the ground almonds, honey, orange zest and crushed cardamom seeds in a food processor. Whisk the egg white until thick. Add the whisked egg white to the almond mixture in the food processor and, using the pulse button, pulse-process until the mixture forms a firm paste. Refrigerate for 30 minutes to make the mixture easier to handle.

Using your hands, roll the almond mixture into walnut-sized balls. Roll these in flaked almonds or pine nuts. Place the coated balls on the prepared baking tray, leaving 3cm between each ball to allow for expansion.

Bake until golden brown, about 15 minutes. Cool on wire rack.

VARIATION

Add 2 tablespoons rosewater or orange flower water when you blend the ground almonds and honey, and add an extra 3 minutes to the cooking time.

persian biscuits

It was a great privilege to hear first-hand about Iran from our student Aydin: its beauty, its literature, the fields of saffron crocuses, how strong Iranian women are and what it was like as a small boy living through the Iran-Iraq War, with the windows all taped up in case they were blown in by a bomb. When I told him I was writing this book he immediately asked his mother for the recipe for *Nan-e Nokhodchi*, the chickpea-flour biscuits that Iranians eat for New Year. Here it is.

Aydin's mother would normally use oil rather than butter. She also uses roasted chickpea flour. In Iran it is bought roasted but it is possible to dry-roast it oneself in a stainless steel or cast iron frying pan. The flour only needs to be lightly roasted to give a nutty flavour. Bear in mind that, after a seemingly slow start, roasting seems to happen at lightening speed. The biscuits work successfully both authentically with the flour roasted and without; the end result is simply different.

Iranians use a biscuit cutter shaped like a four-leaf clover to produce small biscuits with a diameter of around 3–4cm, but any small biscuit cutter will suffice. Half a pistachio is often placed in the middle.

MAKES ABOUT 36

100g butter, softened
100g honey
1 teaspoon ground cardamom
200g chickpea flour, plus extra for dusting
1 tablespoon rosewater

Preheat the oven to 150°C. Line 2 baking trays with baking parchment.

Using an electric whisk, beat the butter and honey until creamy. Add the cardamom. Using your hands, knead the chickpea flour into the honeyed butter. Add the rosewater to produce a light dough that holds together.

Dust a work surface with chickpea flour and lightly rub a rolling pin with it. Roll out the dough to 2cm thick. Use a biscuit cutter with a diameter of 3–4cm to cut out the biscuit shapes. Arrange these on the prepared baking tray. Decorate the top with fork marks if you wish.

Bake until the biscuits begin to turn golden, about 12 minutes. Leave to cool. The biscuits can be stored in a plastic box for 1 week.

VARIATIONS

— Add 2 pinches of saffron with the cardamom.
— Add 4 tablespoons chopped pistachios to the dough, or sprinkle finely chopped pistachios over the biscuits before baking.

BASICS

mayonnaise

Mayonnaise is an emulsion of oil droplets in lemon juice or vinegar, stabilised by egg yolks, which are themselves half water. This process is given the best opportunity to succeed when all ingredients and the mixing bowl are at room temperature. Should disaster strike and the mayonnaise curdles, all is not lost: rescue the situation by starting again using a fresh yolk and slowly adding the curdled mixture.

Using extra virgin olive oil makes a bold mayonnaise, but substitute sunflower oil for some of the olive oil to lighten the flavour. To thin the finished mayonnaise, mix in a little cream, crème fraîche or water.

My first introduction to Aïoli (see the variation below) was on a holiday in the Alpes Maritimes, in South-East France. The tiny village where we were staying was *en fête*. Two tractors richly decorated with alpine sea holly and other wild flowers were parked either side of the church door. After the service, everyone trooped down to an olive grove where there were tables laid out in a grand semicircle. First, huge bowls of aïoli arrived and we waited in anticipation and delight as a long succession of wonderful vegetables appeared for us to dip into our aïoli: potatoes, French beans, carrots, baby artichokes… A memorable feast and one that can easily be recreated at home.

MAKES ABOUT 250ML

2 egg yolks
Pinch of salt
200ml olive oil
1 teaspoon artisan vinegar or 2 teaspoons lemon juice
Pepper

Blend the yolks and salt for 1 minute in a food processor. Keeping the motor running, begin to add the oil through the funnel. At first, this must be done very slowly, teaspoon by teaspoon, blending in the oil between each addition. When the emulsion thickens, probably after a minute, you can add the oil in a thin, constant stream, taking care not to swamp the emulsifying sauce. Finally, add the vinegar or lemon juice and some pepper to taste. Mayonnaise will keep in the fridge for up to a week.

VARIATIONS

— To make Aïoli, add 3 roughly chopped garlic cloves to the yolks and salt in the food processor at the beginning.
— Add chopped herbs or raw sorrel leaves (minus any tough stalks) at the same time as the lemon. Sorrel mayonnaise is excellent with eggs.

hollandaise sauce

Like mayonnaise (see opposite page), Hollandaise sauce is an emulsion but, in this case, melted butter is used in place of olive oil. Thus, as with mayonnaise, the eggs should be at room temperature. The celebrated French seventeenth-century chef La Varenne used an early prototype, which he named *sauce blanche*, in his book *Le Cuisinier François* (1651). He particularly recommends serving it with asparagus, cauliflower and artichoke hearts. Sound advice.

Hollandaise sauce needs to be kept at room temperature until you are ready to serve it. If it gets too hot, it will curdle; if it gets too cold, the butter will solidify.

MAKES ABOUT 250ML

200g butter, roughly chopped
3 egg yolks
Salt
1 tablespoon lemon juice or 2 teaspoons artisan vinegar
Pepper

Melt the butter in a saucepan over a low heat, then bring it to simmering point. You can also conduct this manoeuvre in glass jug in a microwave oven on a medium setting, about 2 minutes.

Meanwhile, blend the yolks and salt in the food processor for 1 minute. Keeping the motor running, begin to add the hot melted butter through the funnel very slowly, teaspoon by teaspoon, giving time to allow the butter to blend into the yolks between each addition. When the emulsion thickens, after about a minute, you can add the butter in a thin, constant stream, taking care not to swamp the emulsifying sauce. (If the butter cools down during this process, reheat it in the microwave.) Finally, blend in the lemon juice and pepper. If the sauce is too thick, add a little water, ½ tablespoon at a time, until you reach the desired consistency.

VARIATIONS

- Add 1 tablespoon chopped tarragon or ½ tablespoon thyme leaves at the same time as the lemon juice.
- For Béarnaise sauce, soften 15g finely chopped shallot in 1 tablespoon butter, melted. Add 1 tablespoon artisan vinegar, 3 tablespoons white wine (or water), 4 crushed peppercorns and 1 tablespoon chopped tarragon. Simmer to reduce the mixture to 1 tablespoon, then strain. Substitute this reduction for the lemon juice.

béchamel sauce

Potato starch flour is more fragile than wheat flour but it makes a wonderfully smooth béchamel sauce. As well as playing an essential role in the base of soufflés and roulades, béchamel sauce can be flavoured with finely chopped parsley and poured over steamed carrots, or flavoured with nutmeg and spread over spinach and eggs for Oeufs Florentine (see page 72).

MAKES ABOUT 500ML

500ml milk
45g butter
2 tablespoons potato flour
Salt and pepper

Bring the milk to simmering point. This is easily done in a glass jug in the microwave on a high setting, about 3 minutes, or in a saucepan over a medium-high heat.

Meanwhile, melt the butter in a saucepan over a medium heat. Take the saucepan off the heat and mix in the potato flour (unlike wheat flour, potato flour does not need cooking at this stage, and it will lose its thickening ability if it becomes too hot).

With the pan still off the heat, blend the simmering milk into the butter and potato flour roux, pouring it in slowly at first, and whisking or beating hard to avoid any lumps. If necessary, put the saucepan over a low heat if the sauce needs reheating. (A liquid thickened with potato starch flour should not be allowed to boil, or it is likely to collapse and become liquid again. Potato flour is unstable when it is cooked for long.) Season.

VARIATION

Add ½ teaspoon freshly grated nutmeg or a handful of parsley, leaves picked and finely chopped, to the milk before you bring it to simmering point.

vinaigrette

The secret of making excellent vinaigrette rests on two things: the proportion of olive oil to lemon juice and/or vinegar, and using the best possible ingredients. A balance of three-to-one works well for a vinaigrette made with oil and lemon juice, which is a common Mediterranean practice, but four-to-one produces a well-balanced dressing if using vinegar instead of lemon juice – any more vinegar would make the dressing too acidic.

Today, we can purchase superb artisan olive oils and vinegars. True artisan balsamic vinegar bears the name *Aceto Balsamico Tradizionale* and is made solely from grape must. It comes from either Modena or Reggio Emilia, is highly prized, aged for at least twelve years and extremely expensive. (The popular balsamic vinegar generally found in shops is made from wine with added grape must and a good organic variety is very pleasing.) But there are many other artisan vinegars of light acidity to explore, made from wines such Cava, Champagne, Muscatel, Riesling and sherry to offer a fantastic variety of tastes.

ENOUGH FOR A LARGE SALAD FOR 8–10

6 tablespoons best olive oil
2 tablespoons lemon juice
1 tablespoon honey
1 teaspoon artisan vinegar
Salt and pepper

Put all the ingredients into a clean jam jar, screw on the lid and shake. Because the oil and the lemon juice and vinegar are immiscible, you need to give them a good shake again just before you pour your vinaigrette onto the salad.

VARIATIONS

– Add a clove of garlic, finely chopped.
– Substitute all or part of the olive oil with walnut oil, which is a favourite vinaigrette in the South West of France. This is particularly good for salads that include walnuts.
– For a Moroccan dressing, substitute 1 tablespoon pomegranate molasses for the honey and add ½ teaspoon ground cinnamon. This is an excellent dressing for a Moroccan orange, olive and parsley salad.

slow-roasted tomatoes

Slow-roasting tomatoes intensifies and sweetens their flavour. Roma plum tomatoes slow-roast best, specifically the San Marzano variety, due to their deep flavour, dense texture and thick skins. Cherry tomatoes make a good alternative, and any tomatoes will slow-roast well, but quarter larger ones. For best results, choose the sweetest ripe tomatoes in the height of summer. The cooking time will depend on their water content and how much you wish to dehydrate them.

A dollop of Aïoli (see page 256) in a Little Gem lettuce leaf, with a slow-roasted tomato on top, makes a simple and delicious finger food. Slow-roasted tomatoes are an excellent addition to salads: they are lovely in a rocket salad with mozzarella and pine nuts. Or they can be made into *tomates confites* (tomato relish) to accompany cheese (see the variation below). Or simply serve them with basil leaves and olive oil in a dish as a side salad. They complement Taleggio cheese in a roulade filling (see page 135) and can be added to the top of a *Farinata* (see page 50) for the second half of the cooking time. Slow-roasted tomatoes will keep in a sterile jar for a week in the fridge – but they usually disappear long before that. The French like to preserve summer slow-roasted tomatoes for the winter by putting the hot tomatoes in a small sterile preserving jar (see page 273), covering the tomatoes with olive oil and closing the tops.

MAKES ABOUT 200G

500g tomatoes, halved
2 tablespoons olive oil
Salt and pepper
6 sprigs of thyme, leaves picked

Set the oven to 150°C. Line a baking tray with a sheet of kitchen foil.

Arrange the tomato halves on a baking tray with the cut sides facing up. Sprinkle with the olive oil, season and scatter over the thyme leaves. Roast for 30 minutes, then check. If the tomatoes need further dehydration, reduce the oven temperature to 120°C and check again in 10 minutes. Continue checking the tomatoes until they have your chosen level of dehydration – I like mine still quite juicy but lightly charred. Watery tomatoes will need more time at a low temperature.

VARIATION

For a tomato relish, add 1 tablespoon honey and ½ teaspoon balsamic vinegar with the oil.

tomato sauce

Tasty tomato sauce is quick to prepare and will keep in the fridge for up to three days. It complements many dishes – serve it with Spinach Roulade (see page 132), Spinach and Ricotta *Gnudi* (see page 116) and Courgette and Spinach Fritters (see page 80).

SERVES 6 AS AN ACCOMPANIMENT TO A MAIN DISH

3 tablespoons olive oil
3 garlic cloves, chopped
1kg tomatoes, roughly chopped
2 bay leaves
Salt and pepper
1–2 tablespoons honey, if necessary

Heat the olive oil in a large saucepan over a low heat and fry the chopped garlic until golden, about 5 minutes. Add the tomatoes and bay leaves and simmer over a low to medium heat until soft and reduced, about 15–20 minutes.

Take the pan off the heat, remove the bay leaves and purée the tomatoes with a hand-held blender. Season and mix in some honey if the tomatoes are not sweet.

VARIATIONS

– Add 1 tablespoon oregano leaves or ½ tablespoon thyme leaves when you add the tomatoes, or 1½ tablespoons parsley leaves or 2 tablespoons basil leaves when you purée the tomatoes.
– Add 1 teaspoon harissa and ½ teaspoon grated ginger root with the tomatoes for a piquant Moroccan version.

pesto

Pesto is a speciality of Liguria, the coastal region of North West
Italy. This sauce has the capacity to turn a dish of roast vegetables
into a majestic full meal.

SERVES 6–8

60g fresh Parmesan or Pecorino cheese, roughly chopped
2 garlic cloves, roughly chopped
120ml olive oil
20g basil, leaves picked
60g pine nuts

Blend the Parmesan and garlic in a food processor until they are finely
chopped. Keeping the motor running, add the olive oil in a thin and
steady stream through the funnel. Add the basil and pine nuts and
process using the pulse button until they are broken down but the
mixture retains some texture.

VARIATIONS

— To extend the season, use rocket or parsley as an alternative to basil.
— To reduce the cost, substitute cashew nuts for all or half the pine
nuts, and add them to the food processor at the beginning, with
the Parmesan and garlic.

home-made edible gifts

I love receiving a gift that someone has made themselves. It's special and intimate. And there is great pleasure in making some delicious florentines or truffles with love and care and giving them to family or friends and watching their faces light up with delight when they receive them. I enjoy the simplicity of it, too. However, edible gifts take a little planning: what are they going to be presented in?
For pesto or mincemeat, you'll need to collect suitable jars or buy some useful 250ml bottling jars as part of the present. To package nuts and biscuits elegantly, place them in the centre of a large square of cellophane, gather up the corners to create a receptacle and secure with a pretty ribbon, leaving plenty of crackling cellophane above it. A few chocolate truffles look lovely in cellophane but a larger quantity will need a small box that you have put aside earlier, or can be put into a lovely pottery bowl that can be part of the gift.

mincemeat

The word 'meat' in mincemeat does, indeed, refer to the use of meat
in bygone days, but it had disappeared by the nineteenth century. The
complex flavours of mincemeat need a minimum of two days to mature
and mingle, but a fortnight is better. You can store mincemeat in a cool,
dry place for up to six months.

Mincemeat makes a fine large open mince tart – use the mince pie crust
on page 214 for a deliciously light base. Or core apples and fill the
resulting hole with mincemeat, cover with a syrup of honey, orange juice
and a little water and bake in a medium oven until soft. For a Christmas
treat, add 6 tablespoons mincemeat to the Vanilla Ice Cream on page 221,
but be sure you chop the blanched almonds very small, or even remove
them – once frozen, they are like stone and can break teeth.

My son Alex and I would habitually make the Christmas mincemeat
together when he was small. He showed tremendous fortitude in
assisting me with blanching the hot almonds.

MAKES 1.75KG

300g Cox's apples, grated
150g carrots, grated
45g dried pineapple, roughly chopped
90g blanched almonds, roughly chopped
360g sultanas
360g raisins
180g currants
Grated rind and juice of 1 large orange
4cm stick of cinnamon, broken
2 teaspoons cloves
½ nutmeg, broken with a pestle and mortar
1 teaspoon allspice
1 teaspoon ground ginger
90g honey
45g butter, melted
150ml brandy

Place the apples, carrots, pineapple, almonds, sultanas, raisins,
currants with the orange rind and juice in a large bowl and mix. Grind
the cinnamon, cloves, nutmeg, allspice and ginger in a coffee grinder
and add to the fruit in the bowl. Finally, add the honey, butter and brandy
and stir well. Spoon the mincemeat into hot sterilised jars (see page 273),
seal tightly and store in a cool, dry place.

honeyed stem ginger

Home-made stem ginger really packs a punch. It makes a fantastic
Ginger Ice Cream (see page 222) and it is excellent in truffles (see
page 247). The honey syrup is delicious, too; try it poured over
Vanilla Ice Cream (see page 221).

MAKES AROUND 300G

280g ginger root
375g honey

Put the ginger in the freezer for 24 hours to help break down the
fibres.

Peel the ginger by rubbing off the skin with a knife. Then cut it into
1cm slices.

Cover the bottom of a saucepan with half the ginger slices in a single
layer and spread half the honey over this layer. Lay the rest of the
ginger in a layer on top and smear on the remainder of the honey.
Just cover the honey and ginger with boiling water and put a circle of
baking parchment, of a diameter larger than the base of the pan, on
top to keep the ginger under the water. With a good-fitting lid on the
pan, bring the ginger to the boil, then simmer gently until the ginger
is tender and infused with the honey, about 1½ hours.

Remove the lid and reduce the honey liquid by boiling until it starts
to thicken. Bottle the hot ginger and syrup in sterilised jars (see
page 273). Wait for 24 hours before eating to allow the ginger to
steep in the syrup.

garam masala

To keep it as fresh as possible, it is best to make garam masala – an Indian blend of warming spices – in small quantities and store it in a glass jar with a lid. In India and Pakistan, each family has its own special recipe for the popular spice blend. Garam masala is particularly good with paneer.

MAKES ABOUT 6 TABLESPOONS

2 tablespoons green cardamom seeds
1 tablespoon cumin seeds
1 tablespoon cloves
1 tablespoon black peppercorns
8cm stick of cinnamon, broken into pieces
1 nutmeg, broken with a pestle and mortar

Put all the ingredients into an electric coffee grinder and grind until the spices transform into a fine powder. Store in a glass jar.

cooked green mango chutney

The British learnt about chutneys in India. This recipe is characteristic of the British interpretation of the genre: a sweet-sour conserve, highly spiced and cooked until mellow and soft. The lemon juice gives it an appealing sourness and dried fruits provide a contrast of textures. Serve with Courgette and Spinach Fritters (see page 80) or Indian Chickpea Flour Pancakes (see page 49).

MAKES ABOUT 750g

500g small green mangoes
2 tablespoons sunflower oil
2 tablespoons mustard seeds
1 teaspoon fennel seeds
100g mild honey
100g ginger root, peeled and
    grated

4 garlic cloves, roughly
    chopped
1 green chilli, roughly
    chopped
1 teaspoon turmeric
300ml lemon juice
100g raisins

Peel, halve, stone and chop the mangoes. Remove and discard the white pith around the stone.

Heat the sunflower oil in a large stainless steel pan over a medium heat and temper the mustard and fennel seeds (see page 15). When they begin to splutter, add the chopped mango, cover with a lid and cook gently over a medium-low heat until soft, about 20 minutes. Mix the honey into the hot pulp.

Meanwhile, blend the ginger, garlic, chilli and turmeric with about one-third of the lemon juice in a food processor. Add the mixture to the hot mango pulp with the remaining lemon juice. Finally, add the raisins. Increase the heat to medium-high and cook, uncovered, stirring frequently, until it reaches 85–90°C, about 5 minutes.

Bring to the boil and boil for 2 minutes, then pour into hot sterilised jars (see page 273), leaving 5mm at the top of each jar clear for the vacuum. Screw on the lids firmly and leave to stand, upside-down, for 48 hours to allow the flavours to mature. Store in a cool, dark place for up to a month. Once opened, keep in the fridge.

VARIATION

Substitute 600g ripe mangoes for the green mangoes. The ripe mangoes will only need cooking for about 5 minutes to soften. Reduce the honey to 50g.

raw green mango chutney

Raw green mangoes have a slightly perfumed lemony flavour. I make this chutney to serve as a relish. My Indian friend Chandan likes it with her Indian Chickpea Flour Pancakes (see page 49). It is a must for the Indian feast on page 136. While it is mixing cultures, this chutney goes beautifully with Courgette and Spinach Fritters (see page 80). If there is any chutney left over, it will keep for a day in the fridge.

SERVES 4 AS A RELISH TO ACCOMPANY A MEAL

2 small green mangoes
2 green chillies, deseeded and roughly chopped
1 garlic clove
Small handful of coriander, leaves picked
½ teaspoon salt
45ml water

Peel, halve and stone the mangoes and remove and discard the white pith around the stone. Chop up the mangoes into small pieces.

Process all the ingredients in a food processor, using the pulse button to give the mixture some texture. Serve within half an hour.

quick tomato chutney

This fresh relish goes well with an Indian meal of a variety of dishes and is best served as soon as it is made, but will keep it in the fridge for a day. It is great with Pakora (see page 137) and Dal (see page 142).

SERVES 4 AS A RELISH TO ACCOMPANY A MEAL

300g tomatoes
2 green chillies, deseeded and roughly chopped
1cm piece of ginger root, grated
2 garlic cloves, roughly chopped
½ teaspoon ground cumin
3 tablespoons lemon juice
1 tablespoon honey
½ teaspoon salt
Small handful of coriander, leaves picked

Process all the ingredients in a food processor until smooth.

bottled fruit and vegetables

Our neighbours in the village of Marnaves in South-West France are devoted to bottling their prime, freshly harvested home-grown fruit and vegetables for the winter. One neighbour, Maryse, explained how, when freezers came into fashion, everyone switched to freezing, but soon realised that bottling preserved the summer flavours much better, so reverted to the method invented by Nicolas Appert, a nineteenth-century Parisian confectioner. He discovered that if food is sealed in a glass container, then heated in boiling water for an appropriate length of time, it remains preserved for many months.

In Britain we talk about bottling and bottled fruit, although we use wide-necked jars; Americans refer to canning, although glass jars are also used. Choose ripe fruits and vegetables to bottle but tend towards under ripe, never over ripe. Below, I outline the preserving process.

FOOD SAFETY: THE 'FOUR SPOILERS'

There are important rules of food safety involved in bottling fruit and vegetables. Food decays, and this is due to the 'four spoilers': enzymes, moulds and fungi, bacteria and yeasts. So it is vital:

— to use fruit and vegetables that are clean and in prime condition
— that the jars and their lids are sterile and in good condition; replace any rubber rings that are imperfect
— that the fruit or vegetables are boiled for long enough to kill any of the 'four spoilers'.

Finally, common sense comes into it: when you open your preserves, throw them away if you see any mould, if they smell 'off' or if they fizz. You should be able to hear the air-tight seal make a clear pop when you break it when opening the jar.

PRESERVING JARS: SPRING CLIP AND SCREW BAND

There are two types of wide-neck jars used for preserving: one with clips and the other with a screw-band. The metal spring clip allows the steam to escape whilst being boiled in the water bath (see opposite page), so can be sealed once filled. But the screw-band jars should not be completely screwed up until after the water bath, so the steam can escape. This is probably best gauged by tightening up the lid completely, then loosening it by a turn of about 3cm before it goes into the water bath.

Jam jar lids for chutneys must have a rubber ring embedded round the inside edge of the lid for a good seal, as in commercial jam jar lids.

There are three easy methods for sterilising clean jars (use either method two or three for bottles with a metal spring clip):

— in a microwave oven: fill the jars one-quarter full of water and heat in the microwave on a high setting. Let the water boil for a couple of minutes, then drain and dry on a clean cooling tray.
— in an oven: clean the jars, rinse them thoroughly, then stand them upside-down in the oven preheated to 140°C for 20 minutes.
— in a large pan: fill with boiling water and boil the jars for 10 minutes.

To sterilise metal lids, submerge in boiling water for 10 minutes, then drain and place facing downwards on a clean rack to dry. (Jars with glass lids attached by a metal spring clip are sterilised with their jars.)

FILLING STERILISED JARS

Fill jars with the food to be preserved while the jars are still warm. In the water bath method (see below), the heat and the vacuum preserve the fruit, not any added syrup. Raw fruit shrinks when heated, so when bottling raw fruit, you can fill it to the top of the jar as a vacuum is created naturally, and there will be a significant space in the jar when it cools. But if bottling cooked (ie. already-shrunken) fruit or vegetables, a space for the vacuum must be created when filling the jar, by leaving a gap of 1.5cm depth between the top of the jar and the contents.

Use a sterilised chopstick to move the contents into the best positions in the jar and to release air bubbles. Before sealing, rotate the jar and give it a sharp tap to release trapped air, then put on the lid immediately.

WATER BATH METHOD

There are various methods for preserving fruit and vegetables. I use a 'water bath'. For this you need a large pan with sides that are high enough submerge the jars. I use a pan of a 27cm diameter, that is 20cm high, in which four 750ml jars fit snugly. To preserve, place the filled jars in the pan and cover with warm water (38°C). Bring to the boil slowly, to avoid shattering the glass. Once it reaches boiling point, boil for the amount of time given in the recipes on the next pages. This varies depending on the acidity of the fruit or vegetables to be conserved. The bottles need to fit in the pan neatly so they do not bang against one another during boiling. One friend resourcefully uses rocks from her garden to separate them; a tea towel works well.

When the time is up, remove the jars from the pan, tighten the tops of the screw-band jars and cool on a tea towel. My French friends leave the jars turned upside-down, which encourages a good seal.

After the water bath treatment, once the jars are completely cool, it is important to check that each seal is airtight. (I leave the jars upside-down overnight before I perform this ritual.) Do this by undoing the clips or unscrewing the screw-band lid, then carefully test if you can lift the jar up by its lid. If you can, the seal is good. Then you can do up the clips or screw on the screw-band and store the jar in a cool, dark place. If it fails the test, either eat the contents straight away or repeat the entire preserving process. Preserved fruit or vegetables with a sound seal will keep for a year; after that they lose flavour and texture.

Fruit can be bottled whole or stoned, in syrup or without, raw or precooked and at boiling point. Use small fruit when you are bottling them raw as they pack more closely.

RAW APRICOTS

I bottle small apricots whole and raw to preserve their tangy flavour. Pack into warm sterilised 750ml jars as tightly as you can without damaging them, filling the jars to the brim. Now follow the jar filling and closing, water bath, cooling and seal-checking processes as described above, boiling the jars for 25 minutes.

Remove the jars from the pan and place either on a wooden surface or on a tea towel. Tighten any screw bands. Leave overnight until completely cool before checking the seal and storing.

To serve, heat the apricots in a syrup of 100g honey and 250g water per 750ml jar. When heated through, lift the apricots out of the pan and onto the serving dish with a slotted spoon. Then reduce the syrup by about 50ml before pouring it over the apricots and serving them.

RAW PEACHES IN SYRUP

Choose small peaches that are ripe but with firm flesh. It is not essential to remove the skins for bottling. If you wish to do so, blanch the whole peaches for 30 seconds, plunge into icy water, then rub off the skins. If the skins do not come off immediately, repeat the process.

Use 650g peaches per 750ml jar. Halve and stone the raw peaches, placing them in acidulated water (50ml lemon to 500ml water) as you cut them to guard against colour loss. Pack them tightly, cut-side down, into warm sterilised 750ml jars, filling the jars to the brim. I like to add a couple of rose geranium leaves or a vanilla pod in between the peach halves. Release any trapped air using sterilised chopstick (see above). Prepare a syrup of 250ml water and 150g honey per jar. Boil for one minute. Immediately add the syrup to the fruit and, again, ease out any air pockets. Now follow the jar closing, water bath, cooling and seal-checking processes as described above, boiling the jars for 25 minutes.

In Marnaves we gather *gratis* an abundance of tiny dark purple wild plums, called *prunes de cochons* (pigs' plums) which bottle wonderfully. They are slightly larger than damsons and very sweet. Any tasty plums, such as Victoria, make an excellent substitute. Damsons are also good, but you need to increase the amount of honey used. I bottle the whole plum because their stones impart extra flavour. To retain their tang, I bottle them with just a little honey added, to enhance their sweetness. Then, when I heat them up to serve them, I taste to test them for sweetness and add a bit more honey if necessary.

For every 750ml jar, place 750g plums and 75g honey in a pan over a medium heat and bring to the boil. Boil for 10 minutes. Carefully pour the boiling plums into warm sterilised jars, leaving a space of 1.5cm between the top of the jar and the plums. Now follow the jar closing, water bath, cooling and seal-checking processes as described above, boiling the jars for 10 minutes.

BOTTLED TOMATO PURÉE

Roma and specifically San Marzano tomatoes make the best tomato sauce because their water content is relatively low. Roughly chop the tomatoes and bring to the boil in a large pan. Simmer until reduced to a thick consistency. Blitz with a hand-held blender. Bring the tomato purée back to the boil and boil for 5 minutes. Carefully pour it into warm sterilised 750ml jars, leaving a space of 1.5cm between the top of the jar and the boiling purée. Rotate the jar to release any air. Now follow the jar closing, water bath, cooling and seal-checking processes as described above, boiling the jars for 10 minutes.

BOTTLED FRENCH BEANS

Owing to the low acidity of vegetables (they are above the critical 4.6pH value) it is recommended that French beans should be bottled using a pressure canner, which raises the heat to 115°C and, thereby, kills any botulism spores.

However, Le Parfait (leparfait.com), the manufacturer of sterilising jars, gives an alternative recipe. Top and tail about 550g French beans per 750ml jar. Blanch the beans in boiling water for 5 minutes, then drain. Immediately plunge the beans into iced water to cool them and preserve their colour, then drain once again. Place the beans vertically into warm sterilised jars, squeezing them gently together, and fill the jars two-thirds full with salted water (using ½ teaspoon salt per 250ml water). Follow the jar closing, water bath, cooling and seal-checking processes as described above, boiling the jars for 1¼ hours.

To serve: rinse the beans and cook them in butter and garlic (see page 172, but without steaming the beans).

quiche crust

A fellow National Childbirth Trust mother gave me this recipe when the class reunited proudly to show off their firstborns – in my case, Sam, this book's photographer. Over the years, it has proved to be invaluable. Potato and olive oil make a light, crisp crust that offsets a creamy quiche filling beautifully. Family and friends often say they prefer it to shortcrust pastry. The recipe yields enough crust mixture to line a 28cm tart dish; use two-thirds of the quantity for a 22cm dish.

ENOUGH FOR A 28CM TART DISH

Butter, for greasing
750g waxy potatoes, grated

90ml olive oil
Salt and pepper

Preheat the oven to 180°C. Butter a 28cm quiche dish.

It is essential to wash the starch out of the grated potato and dry it thoroughly. Put the potato in a bowl of cold water. Fish out one-third of it at a time with a sieve and squeeze out the water from each sieveful with your hands, then roll it up in a tea towel to squeeze out any remaining water.

Place the potato in a mixing bowl, mix in the olive oil and season.

Cover the base and sides of the prepared dish with the mixture. Bake until lightly browned and starting to become crispy, about 10 minutes. (It will continue to cook when returned to the oven with the filling.)

sweet tart crust

The almonds and honey make this tart crust delicious. Press it into the dish as it does not roll out. Vary the amount of honey according to the filling, reducing or increasing it according to the sweetness of the filling. The recipe yields enough crust mixture to line a 28cm tart dish; use two-thirds of the quantity for a 22cm dish.

ENOUGH FOR A 28CM TART DISH OR 28CM × 38CM BAKING TRAY

120g butter, softened
120g potato flour

120g ground almonds
120g mild honey

Combine the softened butter, potato flour, almonds and honey in a food processor. Press the mixture thinly over your chosen dish.

breton buckwheat pancakes

Buckwheat pancakes freeze well between layers of baking parchment; let them thaw out slowly over two to three hours. Nowadays, Breton savoury *galettes au sarrasin* are garnished with a wide range of fillings and served with delicious dry Breton cider. Sweet Normandy buckwheat crêpes are traditionally filled with apple and Calvados.

MAKES AT LEAST 12 SMALL PANCAKES

60g buckwheat flour	1 tablespoon oil
2 eggs	Salt and pepper
300ml milk	30g melted butter

Whisk the flour, eggs, milk and oil in a bowl and season to taste. Place a 20cm non-stick frying pan on a medium-high heat. When hot, lightly smear the pan with a little of the butter. Ladle in 40ml batter and swirl to cover the base of the pan evenly. Cook one side of the pancake until lightly browned and coming away from the pan, about 2–3 minutes. Turn it over and fry until the second side is cooked, about 45 seconds. Make a pile of pancakes on a plate.

SAVOURY FILLING SUGGESTIONS, EACH FOR 6 PANCAKES

— Roquefort and pear with crème fraîche: cut 2 cored Comice pears into 2cm cubes. Line 2 large baking trays with buttered baking parchment and lay 3 pancakes on each tray. Divide the pear between the pancakes, crumble over 120g Roquefort, add 1 tablespoon crème fraîche on top of each pancake, then fold in the edges to form a square. Bake at 210°C until the pears are hot and begin to soften and the Roquefort melts.
— Goats' brie cheese and tomatoes: mix 6 spring onions (sliced and fried in 1 tablespoon butter), 300g goats' brie (cut in 2cm cubes) and 6 tablespoons Slow-roasted Tomatoes (see page 260). Prepare 2 baking trays as above, divide the filling between the pancakes, top each with 1 tablespoon crème fraîche, then fold in and bake as above until the brie begins to melt.

FOR 6 CRÊPES NORMANDES

Peel, core and chop 800g Cox's apples. Sauté over a medium heat in 50g butter with 3 tablespoons each of lemon juice and honey until soft, about 6 minutes. Take off the heat, add 100g whipped cream, 3 tablespoons toasted flaked almonds and 2 tablespoons Calvados. Place a crêpe in a frying pan over a low heat with a sixth of the filling across the middle. Heat through, then roll up and serve. Repeat with the remaining pancakes and filling.

bibliography

BOOKS TO WHICH I RETURN REPEATEDLY:

Abensur, Nadine
The Cranks Bible (paperback edition) Weidenfeld & Nicolson, 2002
Brilliant for students: I have given this book to more people than any other.

David, Elizabeth
French Provincial Cooking Reissue, Grub Street, 2007
For me, a classic. I read it cover to cover when I was living in Toledo.

Geddes, Fiona, ed.
The New Covent Garden Soup Company's Book of Soups:
New, Old and Odd Recipes Boxtree Ltd, 1998
Great inspiration for soups.

Grigson, Jane
Good Things Michael Joseph, 1973
Jane Grigson's Fruit Book Michael Joseph, 1982
Jane Grigson's Vegetable Book Michael Joseph, 1978

Roden, Claudia
A New Book of Middle Eastern Food Penguin Books, 1986
Arabesque, A Taste of Morocco, Turkey & Lebanon Penguin Books, 2005
Invitation to Mediterranean Cooking Macmillan, 1998
Picnics and Other Outdoor Feasts Grub Street, rev. 2001
The Book of Jewish Food Penguin Books, 1999
The Food of Italy (updated edition) Square Peg, 2014
The Food of Spain Penguin Books, 2012

Jane Grigson and Claudia Roden are my favourite cookery writers. I love
the way they tell the stories of their recipes and add apt quotations.

REFERENCE BOOKS:

Davidson, Alan
The Oxford Companion to Food OUP, 1999 (2/2006 ed. Tom Jaine)
A remarkably wide-ranging and comprehensive book that has
won many awards.

Evelyn, John
Acetaria, a Discourse of Sallets 1699, (modern edition Christopher
Driver and Tom Jaine Blackawton, Prospect Books, 2005)

Gerarde, John
The Herball of Generall Historie of Plantes 1597 (modern version Marcus
Woodward *Leaves from Gerard's Herball: Arranged for Garden Lovers*
Dover Publications, 1969)

La Varenne, François Pierre Sieur de
Le Cuisinier François 1651 (modern translation and commentary
Terence Scully *La Varenne's Cookery* Prospect Books, 2006)

McGee, Harold
*McGee on Food and Cooking, an Encyclopedia of Kitchen Science,
History and Culture* Hodder and Stoughton Ltd, 2004
A fascinating and valuable book written for the layman by a physicist.

Pinkard, Susan
A Revolution in Taste: the Rise of French Cuisine 1650–1800
CUP, 2009
A first-rate history of the pre-Revolutionary development of French cuisine.

Pollan, Michael
Food Rules: An Eater's Manual Penguin Books, 2010
A pithy book that boils down to this: 'Eat food. Not too much. Mostly plants'.

OTHER SOURCES AND INSPIRATIONS:

Barnadou, Jacques
Toutes Les Conserves Loubatièrs, 2009

Caldesi, Katie and Giancarlo
The Gentle Art of Preserving Kyle Books, 2013

Corbin, Pam
River Cottage Preserves Handbook Bloomsbury Publishing, 2008

Clark, Sam and Sam
Moro, the Cookbook Ebury Press, 2001

Daley, Simon with Roshan Hirani
Cooking with my Indian Mother-in-law Pavilion Books, 2008

Diacono, Mark
The River Cottage Veg Patch Handbook Bloomsbury, 2009
A great resource to assist in the growing of vegetables.

Duffy, Nikki
The River Cottage Herb Handbook Bloomsbury, 2012

Jaffrey, Madhur,
Eastern Vegetarian Cooking Jonathan Cape, 1983

Ottolenghi, Yotam
Plenty Ebury Press, 2010
Plenty More Ebury Press, 2014

index

For Andrew and my three sons: Sam, Alex and Louis, who bounced through their 'grain-free vegetarian' youth – from all of whom I learn so much, with heartfelt thanks for your generous and varied contributions to this book.

And to my many students, who have played such a central rôle in my life, and their frequent reminder of: 'when is your cookery book coming out?'

A big thank you to Claudia Roden for sharing invaluable insights into cookery book writing with me over lunch at the Hay Festival. And for her generosity in saying: 'you have my permission to use any of my recipes' when I plucked up courage to ask her if I could use my version of her Sephardic Orange Cake. Consequently, I have put in my favourites, mostly slightly adapted, so that you can share them, too.

Huge thanks to my dear friends Giovanna del Perugia (I piatti di Giovanna, catering in the Cotswolds), Montserrat Prat (La Cuina, Cardiff) and Chandan Shah, three amazing cooks/chefs who have guided me in their native cuisines of Tuscany, Catalonia and Gujarat respectively, and gave me some fabulous authentic family recipes, too – all handed down in the age-old, mother-to-daughter tradition. Alex aptly named them my 'dream trio'.

Many thanks to the designer Merel Graeve who helped Sam and I on an early shoot, overseeing the photos of the mushrooms-in-a-paper-bag, rolling up the roulade, and the multi-coloured cauliflowers.

Thanks, too, to Tim Soar for kindly taking the photo of the ceps with the girolle, when Philippe suddenly appeared with a kilo of ceps for everyone on our Marnaves summer school and Sam was not around to record the event.

Jane Bingham, thank you enormously for your guidance on Alex's foreword and my introduction.

I'm very grateful to Angela Young for looking after the production of this book. I would also like to thank Wendy Hobson for eagle-eyed proofreading and Ruth Ellis for a superb index.

But this book would not exist without the talents, expertise and support of Simon Daley and Salima Hirani of Giraffe Books. I met Salima, my genius editor, by happy coincidence at a family party. And she introduced Sam and me to Simon, who came down to Cardiff to work with Sam to shoot the pictures in the beautiful natural light of our music room bay window, using my favourite pottery that I have collected over the years. Simon, your design throughout the book is both elegant and contemporary, and I love the Fournier typeface (appropriately of Jean-Baptiste Forqueray's era). The four of us have worked hard as a team, bouncing ideas off one another and making decisions collectively. Salima and Simon, you are amazing and I thank you profoundly.

FORQUERAY PRESS

The Grain-Free Vegetarian
by Lucy Robinson

www.grainfreevegetarian.com

© Forqueray Press 2015
Text © Lucy Robinson 2015
Photography © Samuel Vines

ISBN: 978-0-9932579-0-2

10 9 8 7 6 5 4 3 2 1

Packaged for Forqueray Press
by Giraffe Books
Creative Director: Simon Daley
Editorial Director: Salima Hirani
www.giraffebooks.com

Production: Angela Young

Typeset in Fournier

Printed and bound in China
on FSC approved paper.